THE RAILWAYS OF

Patrick Howat

The scene at Gilling in June 1960, with 0-6-0 J39 engine 64928 running round the Malton - Kirbymoorside pickup. The station's porter signalman, Gilbert Hugill, is walking away from the signal box. (John Spencer Gilks)

Front cover picture: *two passenger trains passing at Coxwold in the first decade of the twentieth century. (Picture by David Sutcliffe, specially commissioned for this book.)*

Published by Martin Bairstow, 53 Kirklees Drive, Farsley, Leeds, West Yorkshire.
Printed by The Amadeus Press, Cleckheaton, West Yorkshire.

Copyright © Patrick Howat, 2004.

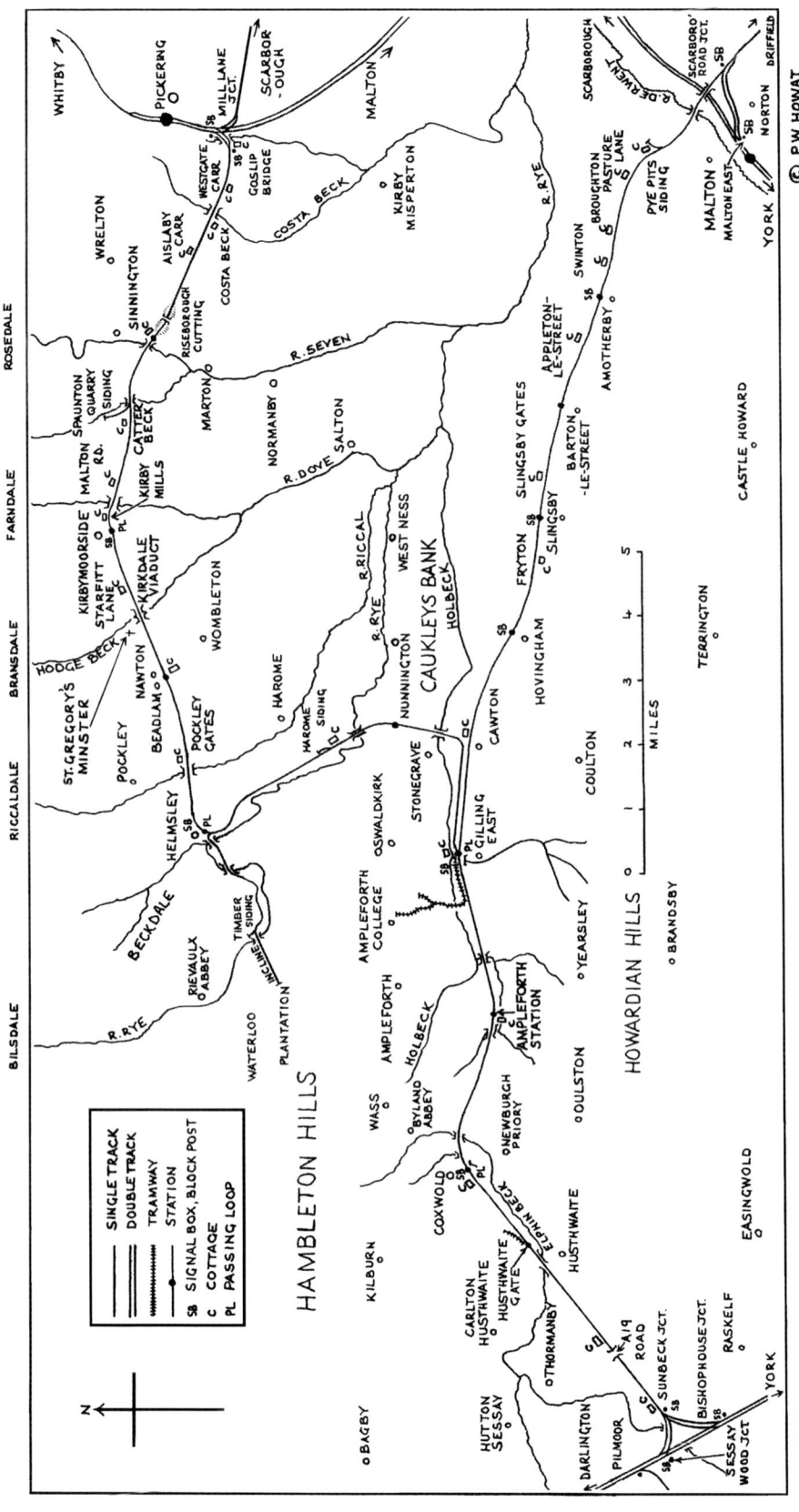

1 - A Troubled Start

The impact of the railway on 19th Century Britain cannot be overstated. Railways were the wonder of the age: they changed everything and everyone. Journeys that had previously taken days now took hours but, more importantly, people whose horizons had previously extended only as far as their local villages or towns were able to travel further afield. As Matthew Welburn, the progenitor of the Railways of Ryedale, put it, a local railway would benefit the tenants of the local estates who were 'at a great distance from markets and who consequently must experience considerable difficulty and expense in the delivery of their various articles of produce'.

The Railways of Ryedale were opened in two stages: the Thirsk and Malton railway (T&M) in 1853 and the Gilling and Pickering railway (G&P) during the first half of the 1870s. The T&M was a product of the Railway Mania when - to oversimplify - many people had more money than sense. It was ultimately built with great reluctance. The G&P started life as a defensive measure and its construction too was undertaken with less than enthusiasm.

York had been connected to the railway map in 1840 when the York and North Midland Railway (Y&NM) from Normanton was completed. In 1841 the Great North of England Railway (GNE) was opened from York to Darlington. The Y&NM's branch from York to Scarborough was opened in 1845.

A long letter appeared in the 2 August 1845 edition of the *Yorkshire Gazette*, from the Reverend Matthew Welburn, curate of Ampleforth. He was eloquent about the potential for a 'Railway Along The Valley Of De Mowbray':

… It is surprising that none of these railway companies should not yet have fixed their attention upon the rich and luxuriant valley of De Mowbray, especially as a railway along this beautiful vale would not only afford considerable and inestimable advantages to the adjacent and circumjacent inhabitants, but it could not fail, as must be evident to anyone familiar with its locality, amply to remunerate those who might invest their money in the construction of a line which would certainly command a great variety of traffic.

The various kinds of traffic along such a line would be very considerable [and] it is to be hoped that this long-neglected, or rather overlooked neighbourhood, will soon realize those facilities and advantages which railways give and which other districts are enjoying.

Within weeks three separate lines had been proposed:

The **Hull, Malton and Northern Union Railway** (HMNU) commenced at Driffield on the existing line from Hull and crossed the Yorkshire Wolds to Norton and Malton, past Hovingham, then north of Coxwold to the GNE south of Thirsk. There was a short branch into Malton and the total length was $43\tfrac{3}{4}$ miles.

The **Whitby, Pickering, Thirsk and Great North of England Junction Railway** (WPTGNE) commenced at Pickering with a junction with the existing line to Whitby. It ran westwards to Gilling, Bagby and a north-facing junction with the GNE at Thirsk. There was a 330-yard tunnel near Byland Abbey. There were two branches both starting near Salton, to Kirbymoorside and Malton respectively. The total length was $37\tfrac{1}{4}$ miles.

The Newcastle and Darlington Junction Railway's **Thirsk and Malton Branch** commenced at a junction with the York to Scarborough line in Norton. It ran west through the Gilling Gap, then north of Coxwold to a north-facing junction with the GNE three miles south of Thirsk. There was a $2\tfrac{1}{2}$ mile south curve onto the GNE near Sessay. The five-mile Helmsley branch had a triangular connection with the main line near Gilling and a 300-yard tunnel through Caukleys Bank; there was another half-mile branch to a terminus in Finkle Street, Malton. The total

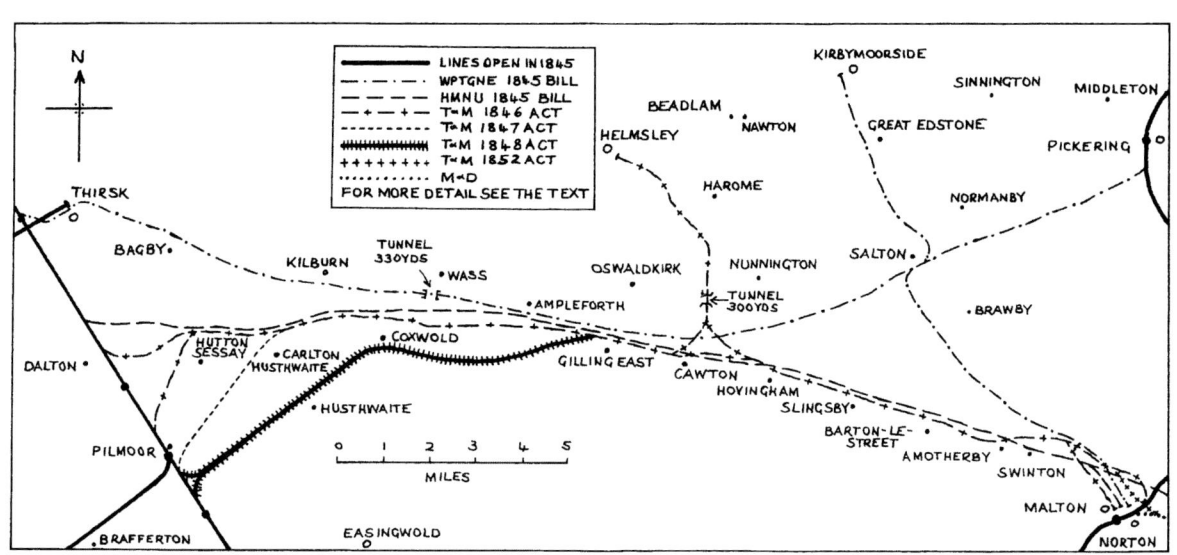

length was 32¼ miles and it was intended to be a double track.

From the outset the T&M received the co-operation of the local landowners. By the beginning of 1846 both the WPTGNE and the HMNU had been abandoned and the T&M's Act received the Royal Assent on 18 June 1846.

The Malton and Driffield Railway (M&D) was a separate company whose route through the Wolds was similar to that proposed by the HMNU. Its Act was passed a week after the T&M's. It had a strong vested interest in the construction of the T&M, for the two railways between them formed a new route from Hull to the north-east, shorter than that via Selby, Church Fenton and York.

In January 1847 the T&M was being staked out but doubt and uncertainty set in almost from the outset. A new Act in 1847 replaced the 1846 Act's original south curve onto the GNE with a 4½ mile line; the Helmsley and Malton branches were also abandoned. Another Act in 1848 replaced the entire route west of Gilling with a new one which joined the GNE at Pilmoor, six miles south of Thirsk. A new short south curve at Pilmoor was authorised by the 1848 Act; had it been built, it would have created a neat triangular junction with the GNE. It was abandoned but an identical one was later authorised and was opened in 1871.

The contrast between the optimism that followed the passing of the original 1846 Act and the dithering over the line's route is striking. In 1847 the Newcastle and Darlington Junction Railway was merged with the GNE to form the York and Newcastle Railway, and in 1848 this in turn was merged with the Newcastle and Berwick Railway to form the York, Newcastle and Berwick Railway (YN&B). In August 1848 T.E. Harrison, the YN&B's Engineer, told Sir William Worsley of Hovingham that 'nothing has been finally settled as to the time for commencing the Thirsk and Malton branch or do I think anything will be settled until the harvest is in and the affairs of this country as well as the Continent appear in a more settled state'.

Following the disgrace of George Hudson in 1849 the YN&B lost interest in the T&M and several other proposed lines. The landowners who had supported the T&M in 1845 eventually realised that the YN&B would not build the T&M unless compelled. On 21 January 1851 Sir William Worsley, on their behalf, served a notice 'requiring the company to proceed with the construction of the Thirsk and Malton branch' and threatening that if it did not do so he would obtain a writ of Mandamus against the company from the Court of Queen's Bench to compel them to do so.

Meanwhile, construction of the M&D had been started immediately on the passing of its Act in 1846 but was suspended in 1847. In 1849 the M&D was on the verge of bankruptcy and its Board felt betrayed: 'they had a right to assume... that the Malton and Thirsk branch, belonging to so powerful a Company, would by now have been completed.' In January 1851 the M&D Board was considering, 'either alone or with some influential interests, applying to Parliament for power to construct the line from Malton to Thirsk as an extension.' Crucially they realised that only by contributing some of their own capital could they persuade the YN&B to build the T&M.

The five-year time limit imposed by the 1846 Act for the construction of the T&M was due to expire in July 1851 and, if the powers had lapsed, a completely new Act would have been required. In June that year the landowners obtained their writ of Mandamus. The YN&B thereafter adopted a more positive attitude and entered into negotiations with the M&D and the landowners. It was estimated that the T&M could be constructed for between £90,000 and £100,000. The YN&B agreed to contribute £50,000 on the basis that it would retain half the profits of the line. The rest of the capital was to be raised by other parties who would be entitled to the other half of the profits. The landowners contributed £15,650, and £35,000 came from the M&D. The YN&B sensibly added the rider that the land should not cost more than £20,000, thus placing an onus on the landowners to be reasonable in the valuation of their land. The agreement required separate accounting for the T&M's revenue and costs. It was explained to a later meeting of the YN&B's shareholders that 'the other parties to the construction of that railway were to take dividend, not according to the ordinary dividend of the company, but such dividend as the Thirsk and Malton might produce, a separate account being kept for that purpose'.

The agreement was not the end of the saga, however. The York and North Midland and Leeds Northern Railways were unhappy about the possibility that the T&M and M&D would draw traffic between Hull, Scarborough and the north away from their lines. (The Y&NM owned the lines from Hull to Driffield, Selby to York and York to Scarborough.) Representatives of the three Companies met in autumn 1851 and agreed that all traffic using the T&M would be charged as if it had travelled by the longer route via York. One can argue that in making this agreement the YN&B at once removed the main value of the combined M&D and T&M railways.

A fourth Act in 1852 legitimised the agreement whereby the M&D was allowed to commit its own capital to the T&M. The M&D, using its agreement as a lever, persuaded the YN&B to divert its line to join the M&D in Norton, which created the desired continuous route from Driffield to Thirsk. The M&D provided the T&M with its access into Malton and, as a result, T&M trains in to and out of Malton had to reverse, a severe inconvenience which contributed to the early demise of the passenger service between Malton and Gilling.

After a long drawn-out start to its life, construction of the T&M was at last commenced. But was any other line built so unwillingly?

2 - Construction and Opening

The capital for the Thirsk and Malton, when it was first proposed in 1845, was £300,000. The 1851 agreement between the YN&B, the M&D and the local landowners that the construction cost should not exceed £100,000 required substantial savings. The early abandonment of the Helmsley branch, with its 300-yard tunnel, had already made considerable savings; laying only a single line (although enough land for a double line was bought) made more. Little could be done to reduce the cost of the two overbridges and a deep cutting in Old Malton. There were only three overbridges between Old Malton and Coxwold and most of the underbridges were built of timber. The viaduct over the River Derwent in Malton was to consist of timber trestles encompassing forty-five spans of twelve feet and one of 30 feet, total length 630 feet. Level crossings replaced two planned underbridges at Husthwaite Gate and Ampleforth.

The contractor for both T&M and M&D was the firm of Jackson, Bean and Gow, with J. Gow in charge. Construction was started and in October 1851 the first sod was turned in Orchard Field, Old Malton, by 69-year old William Allen, the steward of Earl Fitzwilliam who owned the land in Malton. By July 1852 some fifteen or sixteen miles had been completed from Malton to beyond Ampleforth. The M&D's Chairman, Lord Carlisle, remarked to his shareholders that 'a more satisfactory execution of work it had never been his lot to witness... which might be regarded as the very paradise of contractors, so even and level is the line of the country through which it proceeds'. Heavy rain at the end of 1852 delayed construction by two months. The *Yorkshire Gazette* reported that, whereas the average 25-year rainfall for November was about one and a half inches, that for November 1852 had been six and one fifth inches. The hope that the T&M, as well as the M&D, would be ready for opening at the end of 1852 was too optimistic. The M&D's half-yearly meeting in February 1853 was told by R. Hodgson of Whitburn, Co. Durham, that 'the cuttings will be finished in three weeks from this date, so that the contractors will be enabled to proceed rapidly with ballasting the remaining portion of the line between Coxwold and the Junction with the York, Newcastle and Berwick Railway [at Pilmoor]'. The meeting was also told that 'the main line between Malton and Coxwold is completed in every respect and in first-rate working order'. William Taylor of Husthwaite, who travelled on the first train, recorded that 'there were no closing times at public houses and when the line was made the navvies drank all night and slept about anywhere'.

The Board of Trade was informed that it was intended to open the line to public traffic on 1 June 1853. Captain Douglas Galton made an inspection on 10 May. He was unhappy with the timber bridge over the River Derwent at Malton and insisted that diagonal ties be added to resist lateral motion. At three stations the platforms had not been completed and he had reservations about the proposed arrangements for working the single line, as well as the track itself. He concluded: 'with a light traffic, this road may answer, but it is not a description of road well adapted to bear heavy engines at high speed, without considerable risk' and 'I am of [the] opinion that the opening of this branch line… from Thirsk to Malton would be attended with danger to the public using the same by reason of the incompleteness of the works'.

In the meantime the ceremonial opening of both the T&M and M&D was carried out on 19 May 1853. The bulk of the *Yorkshire Gazette*'s report dwelled upon the opening trip and the jollifications at the Talbot Hotel, Malton. Only the section of the article pertaining to the T&M is reproduced here:

[Approaching Norton] a long and heavy embankment brings us to the level; by a slight decline the Scarborough road is passed under; a curve and the York and Scarborough Railway is reached and very soon Malton Station.

Instead however of taking this curve, we continue straight northward from the Scarborough Road bridge, at which point commences the Thirsk line up a gradient of 1 in 70; crossing the Scarborough line by a girder bridge and in a few yards arriving at the Derwent, which is passed by a very elegant, though wood, viaduct. We are now in the North Riding, and a short embankment brings us to the Orchard Field. A deep cutting is then entered which divides the ridge between New and Old Malton. The distance of a mile completes the pass of this promontory of oolitic rock, along the foot of which the Derwent runs its sinuous course, and the level of the Pickering vale is gained below Broughton.

The line after leaving Malton continues simply a surface line for sixteen miles. Its route is just below and on a line with the Street towns - a string of villages along the ancient route between Isurium and Malton. The first station is Amotherby, on the Kirkbymoorside road; the next at Slingsby, a large village with a ruined castellated mansion. Two miles onward is Hovingham, a picturesque village with some valuable mineral springs. The line now enters the vale of Gilling and the village is reached in about four miles. Along on the right Cawkless [sic] and Oswaldkirk Bank form the precipitous outline of the basin and on the left the woody heights of Gilling, crowned by the grim-looking towers of Gilling Castle. Further on to the right is seen the Roman Catholic College of St. Lawrence at Ampleforth, beyond which the scenery grows very wild, and the whole appearance of the country ungenerous. The fact is that the summit of drainage between the basin of the upper Derwent and that of the Swale is here reached; and though, as compared with the towering heights of Yearsley Moor on the one hand and Wass Bank on the other, the surface is low and tame, it is sufficiently elevated, and of such a nature to be exceedingly uninviting. There is a station at Ampleforth.

The summit level of the Thirsk and Malton line is here reached. Passing a rather severe cutting, which has an imposing bridge, we are at Coxwold station. We challenge contradiction in pronouncing this village one the most interesting and beautiful in the county. Leaving Coxwold, the line descends by Husthwaite, Carlton, Baxby, Thormanby (where it passes under the Old North Road), and Cold Harbour to Pillmoor [sic], where it soon finds a junction with the York, Newcastle and Berwick line, six miles from Thirsk and twenty three and a quarter from Malton Station. This section of the line, between the summit and Pillmoor, has been by far the most difficult; there are several heavy cuttings and a great many bridges.

At twelve o'clock the opening trip started out from Pilmoor and travelled to Driffield. Triumphal arches had been erected at Coxwold and Gilling, and the train stopped at Hovingham 'to afford an opportunity of mutual congratulations between the members of the several boards of directors and Sir William Worsley, who along with a party of ladies and gentlemen was awaiting the return of the train from Pillmoor junction'. At Slingsby everyone alighted from the train for 'a very agreeable and welcome luncheon, which had by the kind consideration of Lord Carlisle been there provided for them'. The train proceeded to Driffield, arriving at 2.30 p.m. and left again for Malton fifteen minutes later, arriving at 3.45. James Pulleine, George Pullman and T.E. Harrison, respectively Chairman, Vice-chairman and Chief Engineer of the YN&B, attended the banquet at the Talbot Hotel that evening at which there were speeches of mutual self-congratulation. G.T. Andrews, the YN&B's Architect, was present, as was Gow the contactor, who must have been relieved that his work was nearly over.

The additional work recommended by Captain Galton had been carried out by 26 May and the line was finally opened to the public. The actual date of the first *public* train is uncertain. The Board of Trade gave approval on 7 June but at a shareholders' meeting on 30 August 1853 it was reported as having opened on 1 June, with goods trains starting on 21 May. The date for goods trains may be correct but another source gives the opening date for passengers as 21 June, which seems more likely.

In September 1853 the stations were still unfinished and there was 'a want of accommodation for goods traffic'. T.E. Harrison reported to the Traffic Committee in November that that they were being completed, and it is assumed that by the end of 1853 this had been done. The total cost was £104,934 4s 11d, thus slightly exceeding the hoped-for £100,000 maximum. But at last the Thirsk and Malton was open.

3 - Completion

In July 1854 the York, Newcastle and Berwick, York and North Midland and Leeds Northern Railways merged to form the North Eastern Railway (NER); the Malton and Driffield entered the NER fold three months later. In the 1860s the NER had a near monopoly of the railways between the River Humber and the River Tweed. Other railway companies cast envious glances at this territory which, as far as they were concerned, was ripe for invasion. At the NER's half-yearly meeting in August 1864 the Chairman, Harry Stephen Thompson, wisely commented that 'it was quite clear that the people who were developing the mining and manufacturing resources of the district … would have railways, and if this company would not make them, others would… Where any projected lines showed any reasonably fair prospect of a good traffic it was wise policy to make these branches…'.

In 1862 a group of disaffected former NER supporters promoted the Ryedale Railway. £33,500 of the estimated £60,000 cost of building a line from Hovingham to Helmsley and Kirbymoorside had been raised. The NER declined to co-operate, other than in providing connectional facilities and working the new line, and the Ryedale Railway died. Real action occurred in 1864. The London and North Western Railway (LNWR) had invested in the West Hartlepool Docks and Railway in the expectation that it would have its own rail access there. In 1864 the Leeds, North Yorkshire and Durham Railway (LNYD) was promoted, probably by the LNWR after its previous schemes to enter NER territory had failed. Although this is not certain, it was the general assumption at the time.

The LNYD was an ambitious undertaking, with 124½ miles of railway, a capital of £1,500,000 and powers to raise another £500,000. The 75½ - mile main line started in Leeds and cut across the Vale of York in a north-easterly direction by Wetherby and Easingwold. It passed through the Howardian Hills by a valley at Pond Head Farm, then crossed a 39-arch viaduct near Ampleforth onto an embankment over the College playing fields (which did not please the College authorities) and through a cutting that would have necessitated excavating 298,691 cubic yards of material. Running along the southern side of the Hambleton Hills it curved left through a 400-yard tunnel at Oswaldkirk, which emerged a few yards east of West Newton Grange near Nunnington. From Helmsley the LNYD used Beckdale for 2½ miles before plunging into a 1616-yard tunnel into Bilsdale. It proceeded for ten miles up that valley, crossing the River Seph no fewer than 49 times in 5½ miles, and bored through Hasty Bank in a 1430-yard tunnel. Finally it ran via Stokesley to the banks of the River Tees and on to Hartlepool.

A 30-mile branch to Scarborough started with a triangular junction south of Helmsley. It ran eastwards along the southern edge of the Moors past Kirbymoorside, Pickering and West Ayton to Seamer, thence through the Weaponness Valley to a new station a few yards from the NER's Scarborough station. Another 10¼-mile branch commenced with a junction east of Kirbymoorside and curved up Douthwaite Dale and Farndale. It crossed the River Dove 73 times in 9½ miles. It ended rather suddenly at Birk Hill below Farndale Moor, with the NER's Rosedale Branch some 600 feet above.

The LNYD's advantages over the NER lay partly in its more direct route from Leeds to Scarborough; at the time the NER's route involved a reversal at Milford junction, south-west of York. (The cut-off between Micklefield and Church Fenton was not to be opened until 1869.) The inhabitants of Ryedale welcomed the new company. A resident of Helmsley, Rob Pearson, wrote to the NER, warning that '...the new company is leaving no stone unturned to secure the support of the principal landowners.... There is no doubt the opposition [LNYD] scheme does meet with great favour in the whole of this district'. The Earl of Feversham was a backer of the LNYD, and its route was intended to use his land for some 25 miles.

Within Ryedale the NER's riposte was to propose a 17-mile branch from Cawton, on the T&M east of Gilling, to Pickering via Helmsley and Kirbymoorside, with a triangular junction at Cawton to allow the branch to be entered from both directions on the T&M. There was a 400-yard tunnel through Wrelton Cliff, east of Kirbymoorside, and Pickering was approached from the north. The scene was set for a battle between the two companies when both went to Parliament in late 1864.

The NER was in a difficult position. On the one hand the LNYD was receiving support from the local landowners. On the other hand its scheme was ludicrous, entailing four tunnels of 400, 700, 1430 and 1616 yards; four viaducts of between 430 and 600 yards and with between 29 and 45 arches; multiple bridges over the Rivers Seph and Dove.

Addressing the NER's half-yearly meeting in February 1865 Harry Stephen Thompson stated that it (the LNYD) 'could only be compared to the old story of Don Quixote and the Spanish windmill. Had the promoters been anxious to select a scheme in which the greatest possible difficulties had to be encountered they could not possibly have hit upon a better scheme... When they come to the Cleveland Hills, which, though not so high as the Alps, yet presented a considerable obstruction, the line was not to be turned away, but was carried right through them'. One can only marvel at the naïveté and ignorance of the writer in the *Stockton and Hartlepool Mercury* in February 1865 who stated that 'the engineering works are free from difficulty and the line will be of cheap construction, being put at £12,000 per mile for a first-class double line'. (The 23-mile T&M had been built for £4,500 per mile.)

The LNYD's and NER's Bills both failed in the 1864-65 Parliamentary session. The NER encouraged local opposition to the LNYD, including the Ampleforth Abbey authorities. The latter were dismayed by the fact that the LNYD was to cleave its playing fields by a high embankment. When they complained, the LNYD told them that they could have a viaduct instead but that its £4000 cost would be deducted from the £6000 they would be paid for the land. They backed the NER, who paid their Parliamentary expenses. The LNYD was opposed by landowners in the Leeds area but, more significantly, its estimated cost was deemed insufficient. The NER was opposed by the landowners in Ryedale, most of whom supported the LNYD. The fact is that, as the local monopoly, the NER was not loved. Perhaps Parliament decided that a few heads needed to be knocked together.

In the summer of 1865 the prospects of a railway serving Helmsley and Kirbymoorside seemed to be as remote as ever. On a more positive note, however,

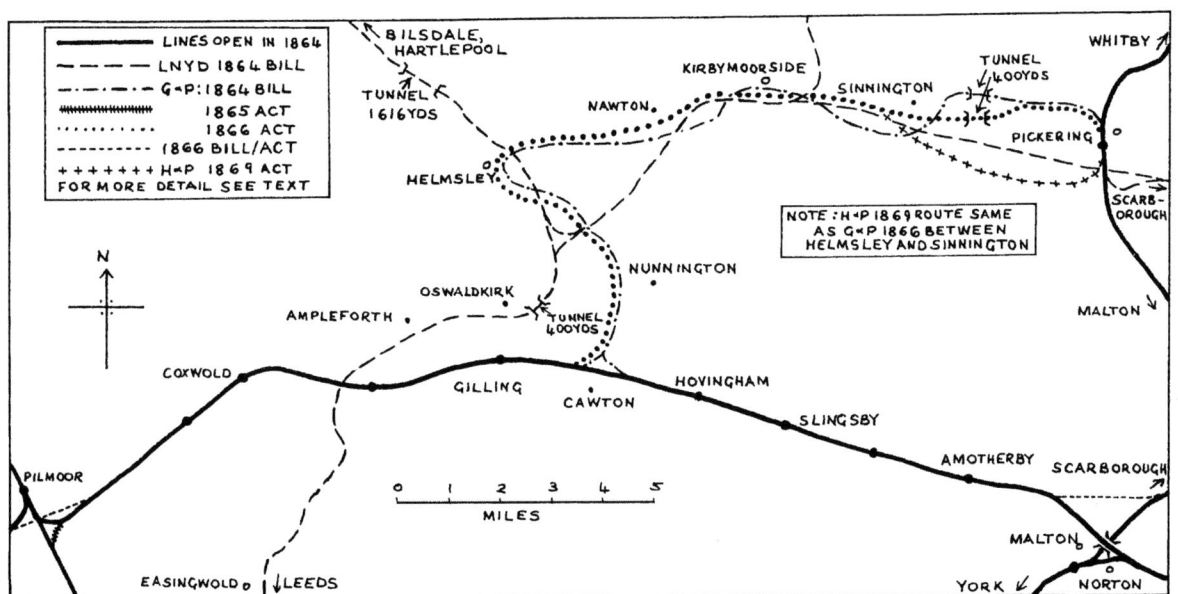

the NER in 1865 obtained Parliamentary approval for the south curve, the Raskelf Curve, from the T&M to the GNE main line at Pilmoor, on a very similar alignment to that of 1848 and which had been abandoned to save money.

The NER won control of the West Hartlepool Docks and Railway in 1865 and this effectively cut the ground from under the LNYD. In September 1865 the NER applied to Parliament again for a line from Gilling to Helmsley and Pickering on a route similar to that of 1864's abortive Bill but omitting the east curve at Cawton. In November 1865 the NER Board and representatives of the LNYD met and the latter agreed to abandon its line. Amongst the clauses in the formal agreement, the NER undertook to make a double line from Gilling to Pickering and double its track from Pilmoor to Gilling; 'quick trains' would be provided between Helmsley and York; and Helmsley would be provided with a 'first class station for passengers (including first and second class waiting rooms for ladies)'.

Despite the fact that the LNYD no longer presented a threat, the NER's 1865 Bills included a new route from Leeds to Scarborough bypassing York, including a 1½ - mile connecting line at Pilmoor between the Boroughbridge and T&M branches and another of 2¾ miles near Malton between the T&M and the York to Scarborough branch. The second of these was dropped at an early stage.

With the passage of the G&P Act in the summer of 1866, and the agreement with the LNYD, all should have been set fair for the construction of the line. But, almost repeating the anguished history of the T&M twenty years earlier, this was not to be.

In 1867 one of the NER's shareholders initiated a scare about the company's accounting methods. Although it successfully defended itself, the aftermath made the NER management defer its plans for new lines. Initially it planned to abandon the G&P in its entirety. Not surprisingly, this was vehemently opposed locally. The NER modified its plan and hoped to abandon only the part of the route between Helmsley and Pickering. Complete abandonment remained a possibility and in September 1868 public meetings were held at Pickering and Kirbymoorside 'to consider the best means of preventing the abandonment of the Gilling and Pickering branch… and to open subscription lists to raise funds for opposing such abandonment if persisted in'. Opposition was not universal, however. An anonymous person, describing himself as 'one of you' published a broadsheet in early October, in which he addressed all NER shareholders:

Do you INTEND to permit the construction of this costly and most unremunerative line?

Ponder on these facts: the Malton and Thirsk Railway passes through a better country and has the advantage of being a through route. It is 22 miles long, and the capital stock is £50,000, equal with debenture powers to £75,000, or £3,400 per mile.

The Gilling and Pickering railway, if made, would have NO THROUGH TRAFFIC, and it would necessitate an expenditure of £280,000, or more than £16,000 per mile. The works on the Malton and Thirsk to Pilmoor add another £36,000, equal to £2,000 per mile more. How is it likely this railway, nearly five times the cost of the Malton and Thirsk, and without any through traffic, can pay any dividend?

… If the handful of people, in Ryedale, who fume so greatly about keeping the North Eastern Railway to a bad bargain, see a profitable investment for a line through their country, let them subscribe the capital to make it.

… Brother shareholders: the naked truth is that no line of railway should be made with your money in Ryedale. There is no trade to yield anything like a fair profit. Attend the General Meeting, on the 16th inst., at York, and support your directors in the proposal to abandon the line from Gilling to Pickering and, if the line is really imperative, vote for the line from Malton. The difference in cost saves you a QUARTER OF A MILLION OF MONEY, which you may as well spend in a Parliamentary fight as throw it deliberately away in making the Pickering and Gilling railway.

Support the abandonment of all costly branch lines not yet made, as the only chance of retaining dividend on your ordinary stocks. Show your Directors that you will submit to no more wilful waste of money.

(As will be seen below, the forecast cost of £280,000 for the G&P was a gross exaggeration.)

In the event the NER backed away from abandonment. A final Act in 1869 varied the route of the line from Helmsley into Pickering, with a southern approach to Pickering which facilitated the abandonment of the expensive tunnel through Wrelton Cliff.

The line from Gilling to Helmsley was staked out in the spring of 1869. The contractor was Walker Stead, a local firm consisting of two brothers from Kirbymoorside and Appleton Wiske, near Thirsk, at a cost of £21,400 (the NER's Engineer's estimate having been £26,557 16s 6d). Construction was already under way when, in 1870, it was decided that the junction with the T&M should be at Gilling, 1¾ miles west of its divergence from the T&M. The additional £3,500 cost of this was offset by £500 saved by not providing a signal box and signals at Cawton and £100 per annum for the wages of the two unnecessary signalmen.

The Gilling and Helmsley line was officially opened 9 October 1871, although the first passenger trains had run two months before, on the occasion of the Ryedale Agricultural Show at Helmsley on 10 August. The single line was almost 6¾ miles long. There were stations at Nunnington and the grand edifice demanded by Lord Feversham at Helmsley. The Raskelf Curve at Pilmoor was opened on the same day; it was just under half a mile in length and a double line. Concurrent with its opening, the original north-facing T&M connection with the GNE was doubled. The two short sections of double line became single at Sunbeck junction.

The only photograph known to the author of any part of the construction of the Railways of Ryedale: Kirkdale Viaduct, by W. Allenby, probably in about 1873. Several very faded patches have been restored, it is hoped without destroying the integrity of the 130-year old photograph. The method of construction is clear. The overhead carriage is standing above the substantial eastern abutment of the three-arch viaduct; other piers have been commenced. (Courtesy of Charles Allenby)

The extension from Helmsley to Pickering was let to Walker Stead in summer 1871, for £61,105. The section from Helmsley to Kirbymoorside was opened on 1st January 1874, with Nawton and Kirbymoorside stations, and was a little more than five miles long. A fortnight prior to the opening a dinner was held at the King's Head Hotel, Kirbymoorside, when the resident engineer, F.S Kelsey, gave a dinner to the forty foremen on the line. Mr and Mrs William Stead, the hotel proprietors, provided, according to the *Malton Messenger*, 'a most excellent repast in their usual bountiful style, using every endeavour to add to the comfort of their guests'. A torrent of toasts was made, to 'The Master Masons', 'The Gangers', 'The Carpenters and Joiners', 'The Railway Cricket Club', 'The North Eastern Railway Engineers', 'The Press', 'The Host and Hostess' and 'The Town and Trade of Kirby Moorside'. The evening ended with 'a choice selection of songs and recitations… which enlivened the evening's proceedings'. The *Malton Messenger* described the opening day thus:

Kirby station was crowded to receive the first passenger train ever arriving there, and was decorated with flags and banners some national and some bearing mottoes such as 'Success to the North Eastern,' and 'Thanks to our kind friends'. The opening of the line by the arrival of the first train was watched with as much interest as though many of the inhabitants of the district had never seen a railway before - and we do not hesitate in saying there will be a few found there who had not previously seen such a thing.

The *Yorkshire Gazette* wrote that: 'to judge from the smoothness with which the train runs the contractors have done their work well and the same remark will apply to the construction of the bridges which are handsome in design and remarkably substantial looking'.

The final $6\frac{1}{2}$ miles to Pickering was commenced shortly before the Helmsley to Kirbymoorside section was opened. At the deep Riseborough cutting it was found necessary to reduce the angle of slopes at an extra cost of £4,700. In his inspection report Colonel Hutchinson of the Board of Trade stated that 'the traffic is for the present to be worked from Gilling to Pickering, at which latter place there is an engine turntable, but so soon as a short connecting line near Pilmoor junction is completed (now nearly finished) the traffic is to be worked with Knaresborough and Boroughbridge from Harrogate to Pickering, there being an engine turntable at Harrogate. Until this connecting line is completed the Company should undertake to work their passenger trains only with tank engines'. In the event the Pilmoor connecting line, although all but finished, was never used. The rails were removed in 1885 and from 1894 for about 70 years the formation was used for enginemen's eyesight tests.

The line was opened on 1 April 1875, together with Sinnington station, and once again the opening was described in the *Malton Messenger*:

The first train left Pickering at 6.30 a.m. The railway station was decorated with evergreens and flags. All the signal posts were decorated with bunting, and flags were hung across the line. A great number of people assembled at the station, and loudly cheered the passengers of the train as it passed along. In the evening the whole of the employees on the line between Pickering and Kirby Moorside sat down to an excellent supper, which was provided for them, the tradesmen of the town having subscribed the funds for it. There was also a ball after the supper, in the waiting rooms at the station. The tradesmen of Pickering closed their shops at noon to enable their assistants to visit the Kirby Moorside Steeplechases, which took place Thursday afternoon, a special train being run from Pickering to Kirby Moorside at 11.30 a.m.

It will be recalled that the agreement with the LNYD stipulated that the NER would also double the line from Pilmoor to Gilling. The high cost, between £35,000 and £40,000 was prohibitive, but in any case the line's being single had caused no delays, and the average loadings of the trains between Pilmoor and Gilling were 'under half a passenger first class, under three quarters of a passenger second class and under 12 passengers third class'. Although a further attempt to have the line doubled was made in 1899 by Lord Feversham and others, it remained single; history has shown that doubling was not necessary.

With the opening in 1875 of the Kirbymoorside to Pickering section, the Railways of Ryedale were complete. It had been an eventful 30 years.

Sufficient land was bought for the G&P to be doubled, as shown here at Bridge 16, a mile west of Kirbymoorside, in 1964. It never was. (Author)

4 - Description of the Lines

The Thirsk and Malton Branch

In this description the station names are given but the stations themselves are described in Chapters 6 and 7. The T&M commenced at the north-facing Sessay Wood junction at Pilmoor, on the GNE main line six miles south of Thirsk and sixteen miles north of York. From the junction the T&M curved sharply round 90 degrees to the south-east for half a mile to Sunbeck junction. The Raskelf Curve came in here from Bishophouse junction, itself turning 90 degrees in its half-mile length. The three lines made a triangle. The two curves that converged at Sunbeck were double lines from 1871, when the Raskelf Curve was opened. The T&M was a single line for the remainder of its length.

For its first two miles the T&M was without earthworks until it cut through a low ridge where it was spanned by a bridge carrying the present-day A19 road, the one-time turnpike from York to Thirsk. This was of brick with stone abutments and a span of 15 ft 9 in.

Continuing in a north-eastern direction, the line was on a low embankment for nearly a mile, with the only significant arched underbridge, a span of 25 feet 6 inches over Ings Lane from Husthwaite to Carlton Husthwaite. Apart from a short downhill section at Husthwaite the uphill gradient between the junction with the GNE and Coxwold was mostly between 1 in 150 and 1 in 200. On at least two occasions vehicles ran away downhill towards the main line, as described later.

Approaching Husthwaite Gate station the line passed through a low cutting, then over the Husthwaite to Carlton Husthwaite road and onto a half-mile embankment. Approaching Coxwold the line passed through several low cuttings and crossed the Husthwaite to Coxwold road by a level crossing. Coxwold station was partially in a cutting, with a bridge carrying the road from Easingwold over the far end, east of the station. This bridge was entirely of brick, as was the next a third of a mile further on and the last before reaching Old Malton.

Sunbeck junction, with the north curve coming in from the right and the Raskelf Curve from the left. (Author's Collection)

Half-way between Coxwold and Ampleforth the T&M passed its summit at an altitude of about 275 feet, having climbed 200 feet in the 6½ miles from Pilmoor. The line ran east as it approached Ampleforth station and the Brandsby to Ampleforth road. From this point to Old Malton it was a 'surface line' throughout and on a gently descending gradient. The only bridges were modest affairs over various becks at or near Ampleforth, Coxwold, Gilling, Hovingham, and Slingsby. Most had timber decks on stone abutments, which had enabled the T&M to be built for just over £100,000, although some were built in stone.

From Gilling the line went towards Malton, passing the villages and hamlets of Cawton, Hovingham, Fryton, Slingsby, Barton-le-Street, Appleton-le-Street, Amotherby, Swinton and Broughton. It passed through the limestone ridge that separates Ryedale and the River Derwent by a mile of steep-sided cuttings and rising gradients. Two roads crossed over the railway, one the A169, the main road from Malton to Pickering.

Emerging from the ridge the railway ran downhill, curved across the Orchard Field towards the River Derwent which it crossed by the 46-span timber trestle bridge. Having passed over the York to Scarborough railway the line descended by the steepest gradient on the line to a junction with the M&D at Malton Low junction (later Norton junction and then Scarborough Road junction). The Scarborough road crossed the railway by a

T&M Bridge 3, Thormanby Bridge, carrying the A19. (Author)

substantial skewed brick overbridge with a span of 27 ft 7 in, almost exactly over the points of the junction. Trains between the T&M and Malton reversed along the M&D for three quarters of a mile into Malton station.

T&M Bridge 26 over the River Derwent from Malton into Norton. This replaced the original timber trestle bridge in 1870. (John F. Mallon).

Scarborough Road junction, Malton, looking west, with the T&M joining the Malton and Driffield line under the bridge. (Author)

The Gilling and Pickering Branch

The engineering works on Gilling and Pickering's 18½ miles were far heavier than on the T&M. Like the T&M, it was a single line. It started a few yards west of Gilling station and for the first 1¾ miles it shared its route with the T&M. What appeared to be a double line was in reality two parallel single lines and there were periods over the years when it would have been possible to observe two trains running alongside each other.

The G&P parted company with the T&M near Cawton and swung round to the north. It climbed over Caulkleys Bank, the ridge that separates this area from Ryedale proper. At the top of the hill it passed through a deep sheer-sided cutting and under the Nunnington to Oswaldkirk road. With its 42 feet span, the bridge over the railway was sufficient for a double line but the cutting itself was excavated for a single line. The line descended Caulkleys Bank past Nunnington station at 1 in 71 to the River Rye and a three-arched brick bridge with stone facings. By now the line faced north-west past Harome siding until it ran along the bank of the Rye outside Helmsley.

Above:
G&P Bridge 5 on Caukleys Bank, the span of which was greater than the width of the cutting. (Author)

Left:
Gilling Parliamentary junction, near Cawton, looking east, with the T&M continuing straight ahead and the G&P swinging away to the left. (Author)

G&P Bridge 6 over the River Rye near Nunnington. (Author)

G&P Bridge 11 over Riccal Beck, a mile east of Helmsley, photographed in 2004, 40 years after closure, built on the skew and with fine stone- and brickwork, in particular the curved ends to the piers and their rounded cap stones. (Author)

Helmsley is tucked into a corner where the Moors meet the Hambleton Hills. The railway made a tight curve on the south-eastern edge of the town, with Helmsley station in its middle. From Helmsley the line ran in an easterly direction and crossed the rivers that emerge from the Moors: Riccal Beck (Riccal Dale), Hodge Beck (Bransdale), River Dove (Farndale), Catter Beck, River Seven (Rosedale) and Costa Beck. The most significant feature was Kirkdale Viaduct over Hodge Beck. It was built of stone, 210 feet long, with three brick-lined arches, the highest 48ft 9in above Hodge Beck. The viaduct was and remains a fine example of stone masonry, as the close-up photograph shows. Whereas the overbridges on the line were built for a double line, the viaduct was for a single line. Had the line been doubled the cost would have been considerable.

Nawton station served the contiguous villages of Beadlam and Nawton. Kirbymoorside station was on the southern edge of the town.

The final seven miles from Kirbymoorside to Pickering took the line through Sinnington station, adjacent to a bridge over the River Seven. From Sinnington the line climbed at a gradient of 1 in 74 through Wrelton Cliff, the low ridge running southwards from the Moors. This, the heaviest earthwork of the G&P, was spanned by a bridge of three 40-foot arches carrying the road to Marton and Normanby. 120,000 cubic yards of material were said to have been excavated from the cutting.

Emerging from Riseborough cutting the line descended to the final 1¾ miles over Pickering Carrs. The gradient was level, but rose gently towards Pickering. There were level crossings at Aislaby Carr, Costa Beck and Westgate Carr. The final half mile was marked by Goslip Bridge junction, close to the

G&P Bridge 15, Kirkdale Viaduct, over Hodge Beck, the river flowing out of Bransdale. Like the Riccal Beck bridge, it was built on the skew. The close-up shows the finely-executed stone dressing, notably around the arch. (Author)

last overbridge and another level crossing. Finally it swung around to the north to meet the Malton to Whitby line at Mill Lane junction.

The total lengths of the lines, as recorded in the NER's Engineer's Line Diagrams made in the 1920s, were accurate to one hundredth of a chain, or 7.92 inches:

Thirsk and Malton	22 miles,	51.69 chains
Raskelf Curve		35.89 chains
Gilling and Pickering	18 miles,	48.70 chains
Total	41 miles,	56.28 chains.

G&P Bridge 29 over Riseborough cutting. (John F. Mallon)

5 - Unfulfilled Plans

The opening of the section from Kirbymoorside to Pickering in 1875 was not the end of proposals for new lines in the area. The remaining proposals were all intended to tap the mineral resources of the North York Moors. All connected with the NER and were standard gauge.

In October 1873 T.E. Harrison, the NER's Engineer-in-Chief from 1854 to 1888, was instructed to make a survey to ascertain the practicability of linking the G&P with the NER's North Yorkshire and Cleveland Railway (NY&C) north of the Moors. The NER had already tapped the Rosedale area with its lines from Battersby on the NY&C, opened in 1861 and 1865. However, before Harrison made his report in June 1874 the NER was approached by the promoters of the Ingleby, Bilsdale and Helmsley Railway (IHB). Just over 18 miles long, it started at the east end of Helmsley station and swung to the north and up Riccal Dale for five miles. It curved to the west near Cowhouse Bank Farm and plunged into a 2480-yard tunnel into Bilsdale. It followed Bilsdale northwards for eight miles on a route similar to that of the LNYD. Finally it passed through Hasty Bank by a 1,648-yard tunnel before making a junction with the NY&C near Ingleby Greenhow station, half a mile west of Battersby.

The NER was asked to consent to the IHB making connections at Helmsley and Ingleby Greenhow. Half-hearted agreement was given but in the event, when the IHB Bill was presented to Parliament, the NER objected to it. The Bill was lost, although it is not certain whether it was defeated or whether the IHB realised the futility of pursuing it further and withdrew it. With tunnelling amounting to more than $2\frac{1}{4}$ miles, it would have been expensive. No more was heard of the proposal.

The Light Railways Act of 1896 was intended to encourage the construction of local railways at minimal cost. By relaxing the previously stringent rules for railway building in engineering, signalling, level crossings, fencing and stations, it opened the way for lines to be built in areas where they would not otherwise have been considered. Crucially, there was scope for local authorities and the Treasury to provide capital. In the event few light railways were built.

The Act was instrumental in bringing about the last flurry of railway activity in Ryedale. The first proposal was in 1897, by the Lastingham and Sinnington Light Railway, whose plan was to run a single line nearly $3\frac{1}{2}$ miles long from Sinnington to a point $1\frac{1}{2}$ miles south east of Lastingham. It commenced 250 yards west of Sinnington station. Curving to the north it crossed the River Seven, continued along the foot of Howlgate Head Wood on the west bank of the river. A quarter of a mile north of Appleton Mill Farm it crossed the river for the last time. It passed close to Cropton Mill, over Cropton Beck and terminated at Seven Bridge. The cost was estimated at £17,980. At a public hearing at Sinnington on 12 October 1897 the Light Railway Commissioners turned it down because 'evidence did not show that the line would be of sufficient public benefit to justify them in recommending compulsory powers for the construction of the railway'. It was dropped.

In 1900 the more ambitious Lastingham and Rosedale (L&R) line was proposed by the Lastingham and Rosedale Light Railway Co., with authorised share capital of £75,000. It was to serve Lastingham village and make a connection with the West Rosedale branch of the NER. The leading light, and one of the Directors, was Frederic Pope of Lastingham. The NER agreed to co-operate with the L&R by facilitating junctions at Sinnington and in Rosedale but, rather than share the NER's Sinnington station, the L&R was to have its own 70 yards away on the far side of the River Seven. The L&R's single-track main line ran parallel to the G&P for half a mile, before curving to the north. By very tight curves it then turned southeast and northeast away from the River Seven towards Lastingham. East of the village it crossed Ings Lane and returned to the valley of the Seven, passing above High Askew. Remaining on the west side of the river, it continued towards Hartoft Bridge and on up the valley to Alder Carr Lane, a quarter of a mile south-east of Rosedale Abbey. It was $8\frac{1}{4}$ miles in length. A branch nearly a mile long left the main line half a mile before the terminus and aimed for the west side of the valley, where it climbed by an incline nearly three quarters of a mile long. At the top, on the Hutton-le-Hole to Rosedale Abbey road and 600 feet above the river, it made an end-on connection with the NER's West Rosedale branch.

The L&R's scheme required 238,000 cubic yards of earthworks and stations at Appleton-le-Moors, Lastingham, Hartoft and Rosedale Abbey. The cost was estimated at £76,682. The prospectus forecast that the revenue would be divided in equal proportions between passenger, goods and mineral traffic. The passenger revenue was expected to come from the miners in Rosedale and from excursions by people making half- and full-day trips from Scarborough, Whitby, Malton, York and Leeds. There would also be substantial cattle and timber traffic. The minerals would consist of ironstone, flagstone, bricks, china clay and possibly coal. The bricks were to be made using the 'unlimited quantities of shale' along the route. The coal was to come from drift mines close to the route of the railway.

At the local Light Railway Commissioners' inquiry Lord Jersey, who presided, declared that it was 'a much better scheme than it was our painful duty to reject two years ago' and declared that he would recommend that the Order be granted. Frederic Pope became the Chairman of the company and an office was opened in Pickering. The contractor, W. Winnard of Wigan, was engaged. The first sod was cut at Rosedale Abbey on 14 June 1902 by a Mrs Muncaster, but no further work was carried out.

In 1903, the Lastingham and Rosedale Deviation Order diverted the route away from Lastingham, replacing it with a route that stayed close to the River Seven. It shortened the line by about 1100 yards but it also necessitated five additional girder bridges over the River Seven and Cropton Beck. The branch and incline up to the NER's West Rosedale branch had already been withdrawn at the time, saving £9,759. The total cost of the final L&R would have been about £70,000 but it was not to be. Although an extension of time was granted and the company existed until at least 1914, nothing became of its plan.

6 - Stations (Thirsk and Malton)

In these descriptions references to 'up' and 'down' refer to the direction of trains, with up towards Pilmoor; the up side of a two-platformed station was that used by trains going towards Pilmoor.

The T&M stations were a very varied lot, with little in the way of a unified architectural style. In the words of Bill Fawcett in his survey of North Eastern Railway architecture (Volume 2) 'no money was wasted on the stations, nor was any offence offered by them… They were plain two-storey, three-bay houses, drawing a simple dignity from good proportions and decent local materials'. These materials were brick, with the sole exception of Slingsby where stone was used. All station buildings were extended over the years and in their finished states there was a superficial similarity between many of them. There was a widespread use of wood in the smaller buildings: waiting rooms and warehouses.

Five of the stations – Ampleforth, Hovingham, Slingsby, Barton-le-Street and Amotherby – had platforms at two levels. When built, the platforms were virtually at rail level but in 1865 the NER decreed a standard height of 2 ft 6 in above rail level. When the existing platforms at these stations came to be raised it was found that the window sills of the station houses fronting onto the platforms would have been almost at the same level. Consequently a platform extension at higher level was made.

Husthwaite Gate station.

Looking east, some time after 1904 when the house was enlarged. The station master in the foreground is George Nathaniel Peacock. The high platform for the ground frame can be seen, with a cupboard for the levers. (Author's Collection)

The station two days before the end of its life, on 5 August 1964 with the pickup shunting its only siding. Lewis Bradley, the station master of both Coxwold and Husthwaite Gate, is standing close to the ground frame. By then the levers were exposed to the elements. (Author)

Husthwaite Gate

Station masters

John Hodgson *	(1862) - 1889
George Nathaniel Peacock	1889 - 1916
John Taylor	1916 - 1929
supervised by Coxwold	*1929 - 1937*
Thomas W. Shaw	1937 - 1938
William Thompson	1938 - 1944
R. Arnold Slater +	1944 - 1945
Ernest Megson	1945 - 1952

supervised by Coxwold from 1952.

* John Hodgson was described as a gatekeeper in 1862 and 1875.

+ Arnold Slater rose to eventually preside over King's Cross station in London.

Station facilities: single platform, siding, wooden warehouse, weighbridge and weigh office.

Originally it was not intended to have a station between Pilmoor and Coxwold. In 1852 requests for a station on the Easingwold to Thirsk highway - the present A19 - were declined. Husthwaite Gate did not appear in the public timetable until November 1857 and even then it was only a footnote. In both 1862 and 1875, when the NER produced lists of all its gatehouses and their occupants, Husthwaite Gate appeared as a gatehouse on the road between the Husthwaite villages. The first passenger to whom a ticket was sold was in late May 1854. The nature of the station then is unknown; perhaps the trains stopped at the roadside. Even when there was a station it was the most basic, indicating the desire of the NER to spend the minimum. It possessed an open-fronted waiting room. The station offices were initially in the adjacent station master's house, which was set back from the line and separate from the station. The accompanying photograph shows that it was extended: this was in 1904 when two new rooms were added.

Repeated requests for a goods siding were rejected, because the NER claimed that it had no powers to purchase the land from Sir George Wombwell, the landowner. When in 1863 Sir George himself undertook to pay most of the cost, it was granted but only for his and his tenants' private use; if others were allowed to use the siding the NER agreed to refund his contribution to the cost. This happened in 1872. In 1890 the adjoining cutting was enlarged and the siding was extended to accommodate up to five wagons, but there was no loading dock nor coal depot. The siding was accessed by means of a ground frame, which was mounted on a high wooden platform. In 1897 and 1899 a timber booking office, a small wooden warehouse and a ladies waiting room were erected on the platform; later the waiting shed was enclosed, expanded and a stove was installed.

The station employed few people, even in its heyday. The photograph on the opposite page suggests that the staff consisted of a station master and a porter only, although a clerk did go there on a part-time basis at times. It remained a very basic station with a porter, Percy Featherstone, until October 1963, when it became a public delivery siding until closure in August 1964.

Coxwold

Station masters

W. Smith	- 1884
George Smith	1884 - 1919
Francis Bradshaw	1919 - 1928
John Taylor	1929 - 1937
Stan Hill	1937 - 1940
Stuart Hunsley	1940 - 1947
Raymond V. Fox	1947 - 1948
Harry Pybus	1949 - 1960
David Farr	1960 - 1961
Lewis Bradley	1962 - 1964

Coxwold station from the west in July 1961, showing the entrance to the goods yard, the horse dock and cattle dock, and the goods warehouse.
(John F. Mallon)

D49 4-4-0 Hunt Class 62774 The Staintondale on a Pickering-bound train at Coxwold in September 1951. The raked gravel surface of the up platform is clearly shown, as well as the ornate waiting rooms on both platforms. The rear of the departing train to York can be seen in the left background. (J.W. Armstrong Trust)

Station facilities: two platforms, passing loop, signal box, nine-cell coal depot, horse dock and cattle dock, goods warehouse, weighbridge and weigh office.

Coxwold station was close to the road from Easingwold and Oulston, which passed over the railway by a substantial brick overbridge east of the station. When the T&M was opened there was no passing loop between Pilmoor and Gilling but one was made at Coxwold in 1900, together with a new up platform. A plan of the station at that time indicates that a footbridge was intended, but it was never provided.

Coxwold was influenced by the Wombwell family from the nearby Newburgh Priory. The substantial station building was on the down platform and provided accommodation for the station master. The first class waiting room was in the main building, carpeted and with prints of the Wombwell family on the walls. A second class waiting room was further along the same platform and there was another waiting room on the up platform, both timber-built in an ornate style. The up platform waiting room was demolished after the end of the passenger service in 1953.

Commencing in 1895 there was an annual competition for the Best Kept Station, in which Coxwold was a regular winner of a first class prize. Early photographs show platforms with raked gravel surfaces, backed by beds of flowers and bushes. The station's position partially in a cutting, the sides of which were planted with flowers, made it more picturesque. George Smith, station master for 35 years, was the architect of the station's early success in the competition. He even went to the ruined Byland Abbey, two miles away, in search of stone to enhance the garden. About a dozen carved stone faces were brought to decorate a retaining wall for the garden on the up platform, which were still there many years later (as well as several cannon balls whose origins are uncertain). Coxwold remained a station of green-fingered station masters for many years. In 1939, during the tenure of Stan Hill, Bill Wood was sent there as a clerk and was left in no doubt that his railway education would be enhanced by the addition of some horticultural skills, although not quite the ones that he might have expected:

Plants were raised from seed in the greenhouse in the station master's garden. The 'pièce de résistance' was a large bed of salvia and lobelia, with a representation of the White Horse in alyssum as a centrepiece. Later that year the station gained another prize.

One day the station master said 'do you know anything about tomatoes?' My answer was a negative one. 'Well' he said, 'come to the greenhouse and have a look at mine.' So I dutifully followed him into the greenhouse. He closed the door and then said 'have a look across at the house and see if you can see my wife.' He bent to a crate behind the door and lifted a large bottle of beer and, as I looked, his wife's face appeared at an upstairs window. 'Now' he said, 'if she asks you what I was doing in the greenhouse, you say that I was showing you my tomatoes.' Over the next week or two I was to become very familiar with the progress of those tomatoes, and the uncanny way in which the beer crate remained full of bottles of the elixir.

Like many rural railways the T&M had a close relationship with its customers. A story that illustrates this relationship is related by Hugh Wentworth Ping; it concerned his journey from Ampleforth in 1943, returning from naval leave and with an important connection to make at York. The morning trains to and from York were due to pass at Coxwold:

We arrived at Coxwold to find that the train from York had not yet arrived, so passengers got out to chat. The train from York duly arrived but then there was a great commotion. It seemed that someone or something had been left behind at Ampleforth. So they put my train into reverse and went back for it. Many of the passengers were very worried because, like me, they wanted to catch connections. I was sitting there fuming: at my age and in the Navy, you had to be on time and catch the train back from leave. We duly chugged back again to Coxwold, where there was uproar, because this was strictly against the regulations. The train from York went off and we expected to pull out at any moment. But a young boy suddenly said something like 'what about Mrs Somebody-or-other?' They all said 'what about her?' 'She's been down and found the train from York still standing there and the train to York gone, and she thought she'd missed it'. So we waited and they sent this boy haring off up to get her. This old lady arrived, with her bags and baskets, puffing and panting, and her hat all awry, and they pushed her onto the train. We arrived at York and the London train was waiting, and there was all hell to pay.

Lewis Bradley came to Coxwold as station master in 1962 and looked after Husthwaite Gate as well. He and Cyril Sherwood, the porter signalman, were Coxwold station's only staff.

We mainly handled coal but there was timber, occasional horses for a trainer up the road, and wool. We didn't get any sheep or cattle. Farmers in the past had been used to chopping a tree down for the winter fuel. I got them interested in coal and we started selling anthracites, which was a new fuel to them. At one time I had about 25 wagons of coal in the yard. I was getting a bit worried! Eventually they told me to put the empties into store, but I had nowhere to store them. Sugar beet was coming back, on the increase. During the summer the coal trade was slack and the sugar beet hadn't started; but in August I started ordering extra coal so that I got extra wagons for the sugar beet. If I'd ordered extra wagons just for sugar beet, I wouldn't have got them, so I had to order a full one of coal to create an empty one for the beet. I got quite skilled at it.

Cyril Sherwood was porter signalman at Coxwold for many years and remembered the racehorses: 'there was a Major Geipel who bred racehorses at The Old Hall. His horses were thoroughbreds and we had to be careful with them. With the groom we walked them over the line to the loading dock and we used to cover the line with wood.'

During its first years, and until June 1914, the station was also the village post office, with a posting box in the central passage through the station building.

Ampleforth

Station masters

John Ridsdale	1853
Galton	1853 -
Mrs Winsor	- 1862
Richard Winsor	1862 - 1866
William Shaw	1866 - 1887
E. Temple	1887 - 1902
G.E. Milburn	1902 - 1906
J.T. Bates	1906 - 1914
J. Ainsley	1914 - 1933
supervised by Coxwold	*1933 - 1937*
George Kettlewell	1937 - 1945
William G.D. Thompson	1945 - 1947
William H. Johnson	1948 - 1950

Station facilities: one two-level platform, five-cell coal depot, loading dock, small brick and wooden warehouses, weighbridge and weigh office.

Ampleforth station was on the Yearsley to Ampleforth road, $1\frac{1}{2}$ miles away from the village it purported to serve. As far as can be ascertained, it was opened with its two-storey station building. In 1856 a waiting room in a single-storey extension was added. In appearance it was similar to Gilling, with the roof above the single-storey extension sweeping down to provide a canopy over the platform. A siding served the coal depot and another ran parallel with the main line over the level crossing to the loading dock.

Ampleforth station looking east in August 1964. By this time the station had been closed to all traffic for 14 years. The arm of the up home signal on the left had been removed on 17 December 1962. (Author)

Ampleforth never had many facilities, and by July 1961, when this photograph was taken, they had all gone. The coal depot was behind the platform. The down home signal can be seen behind the platform canopy, half way up the cutting side so as to give train drivers clear view as they rounded the bend into the station. (John F. Mallon)

Ampleforth's passenger numbers were never high. From the mid-1920s the introduction of a bus service to York caused a severe decline. By 1938 1669 tickets were issued annually but ten years later it was only 516. From 1937 until 1945 George Kettlewell ran the station with a porter:

Things were very quiet when I first went there in April 1937 but I had an incentive to increase business. As soon as the station receipts reached £750 a year, but excluding the coal sale, a station master automatically advanced in grade from class 6 to class 5. The £750 came in the first year, mostly from the farms. We had quite a number of farmers who had crops of cereals and potatoes. In the days when you had the itinerant threshing machine, moving from farm to farm, it was necessary to keep on hand a stock of at least a thousand sacks, so that, if a farmer got short notice of a threshing machine coming on the Monday, he would ring up on the Sunday and ask for some sacks. We never said 'no'. The result was a pheasant or a pound of butter, or something of that sort, which was very kind of them. It wasn't really necessary as it was my job.

Quite honestly, after being there for six months I was bored to tears. In the afternoon I could safely get the rifle and disappear for a couple of hours, which I did quite often. Ultimately I got a licence from the police and had permission from all the farmers around to shoot rabbits etc. The odd hare used to get in the way and occasionally so did a pheasant or a partridge. We fed very well on them. Once the district inspector was waiting for me, sitting on the station seat, when I got back from shooting; a rabbit helped to straighten things out with him.

Prior to the war breaking out, at Yearsley there was a rehabilitation centre for young offenders from the Manchester and Liverpool areas. They'd all been inside for various periods and they came out for rehabilitation under the auspices of the Ministry of Labour and the Forestry Commission. They worked in the forestry, on felling timber, clearing up etc. When the camp was closed we demolished it, loaded the huts, and despatched them to the north of Scotland. They sent a gang of six men out from York to load the buildings. I left them for half an hour and went up the village and back. When I got back they had loaded a double bolster with the sides of a hut. The loading gauge is 13 foot 6 inches but this stood about 21 foot something. So I suggested that it was taken off and put the other way up. They refused to do this so I told them to take the next train back to York, due in half an hour. So they stayed and got on with it.

The presence of Ampleforth College in the vicinity generated little business, as Gilling station was better equipped and more convenient. What College business passed through Ampleforth station usually happened by mistake. One such traveller was the Belgian Prime Minister, Hubert Pierlot, accompanied by his wife and family. When the Germans overran Belgium in 1940, its Government went into exile. M. Pierlot had arranged for his sons to attend Ampleforth College and the family arrived on the last train from York one night in January 1941. George Kettlewell:

It was a shocking night: the heavens opened, the wind blew and it was the blackout. The oil lamps never were much good even before the blackout: you needed something lit to see if they were alight! It was only because the wind carried my voice as I called out 'Ampleforth' that they heard at the last moment and got out. They couldn't speak English and I couldn't speak French, so it was a bit of an impasse, but I managed to establish the basic facts about them. I telephoned the College Procurator and I looked after the family until two cars came down to pick them up.

On 28 April 1941 a tragic accident happened while the pupils were returning to the College, occupying two coaches attached to the rear of a train from London. As the train travelled through Lincolnshire one of the coaches was accidentally set on fire. M. Pierlot's sons Jean and Louis were among the six pupils who died.

Ampleforth retained its station master until it was closed on 3 June 1950, two-and-a-half years before the other stations lost their passenger service, but trains called at the station on 5 June in connection with the Ampleforth College 'Exhibition'. The goods service ended on the same day. For several years until the end of 1962 the station was a 'camping cottage'.

Gilling

Station masters

Wright	1853 - 1889
Ralph Richardson	1889 - 1891
J.E. Parnaby	1892 - 1894
Frank Wood	1894 - 1916
Tom Barlow	1916 - 1939
Fred Gillery	1939 - 1948
Tom Thackray	1948 - 1964

Station facilities: two platforms, passing loop, footbridge, signal box, seven-cell coal depot, yard crane, carriage loading and cattle dock, goods warehouse, horse stable, weighbridge and weigh office.

Serving the village of Gilling East, Gilling station was situated adjacent to the main road from York to Helmsley. The station house was on the up platform on the south side of the line, and was built of pale bricks; as at Ampleforth, a canopy covered part of the up platform. The booking office was at the end of the station next to the level crossing.

Gilling had the range of traffic to be expected at a rural station, including timber, livestock, animal feeding stuffs, grain and coal. The goods yard was a small one, with three sidings one of which served the coal depot. Part of the warehouse was rented by the Brandsby Agricultural and Trading Association. There were also sidings, known as the College Sidings, west of the level crossing. One of their main uses until 1930 was to hold a Gilling-terminating passenger train while through passenger trains passed through the station. From 1895 the three-foot gauge Ampleforth College tramway commenced at the west end of the College Sidings. (See Chapter 12.)

According to Gilbert Hugill, the station's porter signalman from 1948 until 1964, an unusual method was used for a local farm to communicate with the station: 'Lodge Field farm up on the hill, didn't have the telephone. When they wanted an empty wagon to load their sacks of grain in they used to put a sheet or something out on the washing line. We would see it blowing and would order the wagon.' What happened on wash days is not recorded.

On the opening of the T&M in 1853 it is unlikely that Gilling possessed a passing loop. The loop, and the second platform, were possibly provided on the opening of the Helmsley branch in 1871. In 1906 a 'scissors' crossover was installed east of the platforms to give greater flexibility in working the trains on both lines; it was replaced by a single crossover in 1955.

Below, upper: Gilling station looking east a few years after the new signal box was opened in 1906, with several members of staff interrupting their daily activities for the photograph. (Lens of Sutton)

Below, lower: The scene at Gilling station on 27 July 1964, with a Scarborough-bound diesel multiple-unit standing in the platform, on the last day of passenger trains on the line. (Author)

In 1891 a water tank was installed, with water columns on the up line next to the level crossing and on the down line east of the platform. The source of the water for the tank was the same as for the village's domestic supply. During the Second World War there was increased demand for water, owing to the number of extra trains passing through. Audrey Hugill (née Cooper), who worked at the station, recounted the consequences for the housewives of Gilling East:

Some of the trains had big engines that needed a lot of water and, with them taking water at Gilling station, it was causing an acute shortage of water in the village. On Monday mornings the telephone would ring: the ladies of the village were trying to do the weekly wash but there was only a trickle of water coming through the tap. Mr Gillery, the station master, took the calls, and it got so bad that he had to do something about it. The outcome was that we had two men who came from York with a pump, to pump water from the beck into the water tank next to it, so as to leave enough for the houses in the village. That solved the problem.

Also in 1891 there were complaints about the danger of crossing line by the level crossing when shunting operations were being carried out. A footbridge at Craven Road Crossing, Southcoates, Hull, was made redundant and was re-erected at Gilling in 1894, with a glass bottle containing a coin and a piece of paper inserted into its foundations. When found on the demolition of the bridge the paper provided a record of the station at the time.

The following were the staff and employees, at or about Gilling in service of the North Eastern Railway, viz:

Frank Wood	station master
Edward Pearson	chief clerk
George Cooper	second clerk
John Welford Megginson	signal porter
Ransom Dale	signal porter
Thomas J. Ewing	signal man
Robert Skelton	foreman platelayer
William Seedam	fog signalling and platelayer
(indecipherable)	fog signalling and platelayer
(indecipherable)	pumping engine

The winter service of trains were 28 ordinary passenger, 3 goods in and out, 6.46am to 6.19pm. Summer 3 goods and 34 ordinary passenger trains in and out 6.46 a.m. to 8.19pm.

The signal cabin at this time contained 17 working levers and one spare.

During the Second World War the station was very busy, according to Cyril Sherwood: 'it was wartime and you could relax rules a bit, with these ammunition trains and tank trains and whatnot. You could accept them at caution and bring them up to the home signal. There was a new signalman who had been accepting trains from Hovingham, Coxwold and Helmsley. He had the platforms full, with trains coming up the other lines as well, until he had everything choc-a-bloc and he had to go and get Matt Braithwaite, the usual man, who was at home in one of the station cottages to come and sort it out'.

From 1926 until closure in 1964 the Gilling station master was also in charge of Hovingham, Slingsby, Barton-le-Street and Amotherby stations.

Hovingham station at some date after 1896 when the word 'Spa' was added. Amongst the group of staff is a porter (left), a platelayer, a porter signalman or clerk, the station master - possibly W. Johnson - and another clerk. (Author's Collection)

Hovingham station at an unknown date, probably early in the 20th Century, looking east. The two different heights of the platform are clearly visible. (Author's Collection)

Hovingham (Spa)
Station masters
F. Benson	1853
John Ridsdale	1853 - 1863
E. Lobatto	1863 - 1873
G. Seller	1873 - 1875
T. Abbott	1875 - 1879
M. Long	1879 - 1888
Thomas Waller	1889 - 1897
W. Johnson	1897 - 1922
A. Durance	1922 - 1926

supervised by
    Gilling from 1926
porter signalmen in charge
Bell
Ted Taylor	- 1951
Eric Hartley	1951 - 1964

Station facilities: one two-level platform, five-cell coal depot, carriage dock, cattle dock, two warehouses, small wooden warehouse, weighbridge and weigh office.

The land surrounding Hovingham station was owned by the Worsley family of Hovingham Hall. In 1845 Sir William Worsley had been keen to promote Hovingham as 'a place of considerable resort and spa'; on 1 October 1896 the word 'Spa' was added to the name, presumably in the hope of attracting more business. Passenger traffic was heavy in the early years, behind only Helmsley and Kirbymoorside, but it declined severely in the 1920s, like at all the Ryedale stations.

The goods warehouse was rented by two local corn merchants, John Woodcock and Messrs. Sidgwick and Leefe. Shortly afterwards Woodcock asked for the warehouse to be given an upper floor for grain storage. The storey was not added because in 1857 Woodcock's request for a second warehouse to be built was granted. Inside the original warehouse there was a loading deck and a crane. Latterly this warehouse was used mainly for storing and issuing sacks.

Below, lower: A bird's-eye view of Hovingham station and its yard in December 1964, taken from atop the up home signal. The sidings on the left, originally three in number, were laid in 1863. (Author)

Hovingham was well equipped with sidings. More timber sidings were laid in 1863 close together in the yard, one of which also served a cattle dock and carriage dock. The timber, from the southern side of the village including the Worsley Estate, was brought to the station by horses and wagons. There was also much livestock traffic, 13,925 head being sent out in 1896, an average of 270 per week.

Hovingham's years of glory came in the 1950s when it forwarded great quantities of limestone from the nearby Wath quarry. In 1948 the yard was extended and a new high loading dock was built. The stone traffic is described in greater detail in Chapter 14. Eric Hartley was the porter signalman there from 1951 until 1964:

Sugar beet was a big business, in the season. It was loaded from the other dock, next to the farthest away of the three sidings. We used to get well over 1000 tons in a season. I managed it for the farmers. The farmers used to bring their permits down, when they received them and I had to look after them. I kept a record of all the farmers and how many permits they had. I would ask them when they wanted the wagons. I had to order the wagons and when they had arrived I gave the farmers a ring. I had a special drawer in the office for the permits and I made a graph to show when they were all due.

Slingsby
Station masters

Smith	- 1857
Kirk	1857 - 1882
John Craven	1882 - 1913
J. Easton	1913 - 1918
George E. Wood	1919 - 1926

supervised by Gilling from 1926
porter signalmen in charge

W. Worthy	- 1936
John P. Trees	1937 - 1942
Fred Wright	1942 - 1964

Station facilities: one two-level platform, eight-cell coal depot, carriage dock, cattle dock, two warehouses, small wooden warehouse, weighbridge and weigh office.

Slingsby station was constructed by the Earl of Carlisle, who owned the surrounding land. This explains why, unlike the other T&M stations, it was built of stone. When the Earl sought the £350 cost from the NER he was paid only £300, the average cost of the other stations. Nevertheless the result was an attractive building with raking parapets on the roof gables, stone cornices and, unlike the other T&M stations, a bay window facing onto the platform.

After extensions in 1897, 1904 and 1914, the building housed a general waiting room, a ladies waiting room and a combined station master's and booking office. The ground floor also included a living room, sitting room and kitchen. Upstairs there were four bedrooms and a bathroom.

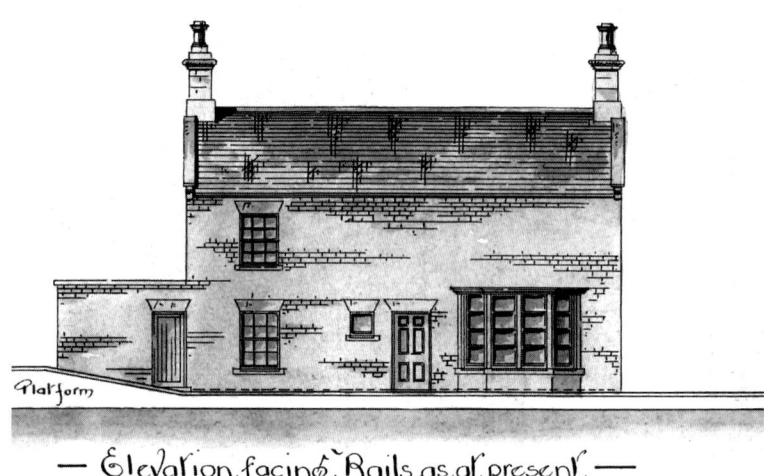

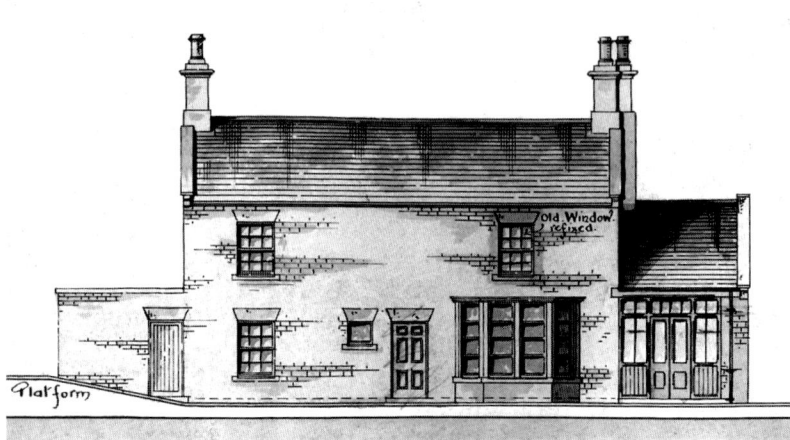

The Slingsby station building was enlarged in 1897. Here we see the architect's before-and-after elevations for the railway side of the building. (Author's Collection)

Right: Slingsby station probably in the 1950s, showing the 1914 extension. Because of the higher platform, the new extension's windows are also higher. A wooden warehouse stands behind the cupboard-like platform signal frame. (Author's Collection)

Right lower: Slingsby and its magnificent three-storey grain warehouse in 1961. (John F. Mallon)

Immediately behind the platform there was a small wooden warehouse in which sacks were kept, as well as small packages awaiting collection or delivery. There was a large goods warehouse but in 1858 John Woodcock of Hovingham asked the NER to erect a new grain warehouse. The result was a very large, three-storey warehouse. Fred Wright was the porter signalman in charge of Slingsby from 1942 until the station was closed in 1964:

The big warehouse had a brick floor. It was a big, lovely space, that. The columns that supported the upper floors were big squared timbers, resting on lead plates on the bricks. The floorboards took a terrific weight. When I first arrived the Co-op rented it. Meal came from Hull, cattle cakes and all that sort of stuff. It was used a lot during the war. At first there was Russian oil in drums on the ground floor. Then later during the War it was cleared and used as a food store: sugar in the two top floors and a lot of Nestlés milk in the bottom. Then the Brandsby Agricultural and Trading Association had it full of corn. Nobody wanted it after that and it was demolished after the station had closed.

Arthur Cook started on the NER as a clerk at Slingsby in 1921:

We had quite a bit of livestock going away. There was one lot coming in that I always remember, from a man farming on the Castle Howard estate. It was the Goathland sheep fair and he brought a lot of Moorjocks in. We had a big road gate shutting the yard off. It wasn't an ordinary five-barred gate but longer and bigger. While he was in the office and we were doing the business, signing for them and everything, I looked out of the window and saw all the sheep going over the top of the gate. They all went and there wasn't one left in the village street when he got out of the gate. They went down towards Fryton and Hovingham.

On the passenger side, we regularly had hucksters, who went round farms collecting butter and eggs and stuff. Simpson from Ness used to call at the station with what he had collected with his horse and rulley. The boxes were quite big, partitioned in the middle and with trays. Then they were sent away to Leeds and elsewhere. We never weighed them as they were always full and always weighed the same. Years ago a family called Lange - it was a German name - farmed at South Holme and came up on a bicycle nearly every morning with two little brown paper parcels of cream cheese which they made on the farm. One went to Borders of York and the other to Rowntrees of Scarborough.

Slingsby had a passing loop for some years, which was removed but reinstated and lengthened in 1943, when ammunition was unloaded onto a specially-made adjacent concrete hard-standing alongside.

Barton-le-Street

Station masters

Galton	- 1853
F. Benson	1853 -
Mrs Smith	- 1874
James Smith	1874 - 1903
T. Parkin	1903 - 1907
A.E. Barrett	1907 - 1910
W. Sewell	1910 - 1922
W.E. Wood	1922 - 1926

supervised by Gilling from 1926
porters in charge

Clayton	
Tom Sharp	1933 - 1935
Jim Sharp	c1937 - 1964

Station facilities: one two-level platform, three-cell coal depot, cattle dock, small wooden warehouse, weighbridge and weigh office.

Barton station had few facilities. Its only goods storage facility was a wooden warehouse on the platform. Its station house was its most interesting feature. Built of a dark brick it was eventually among the largest on the T&M. The original station was a single-storey affair but this had two new bedrooms built over it in 1863. In 1875 an additional room, to serve as waiting room and office, was added. Finally, in 1890 another extension, a rear projection from the main building, was erected. It is believed that one early station master had a very large family and that the wing was added to accommodate them.

Jim Sharp was the porter at Barton for nearly 30 years. His widow, May, remembered the house as being very damp:

We had an outside soil toilet. The washhouse was right across the yard. We had to cross the yard to hang the clothes out. There was no electricity. During the War there was a searchlight detachment there and after they left Jim asked the railway company to put electricity in; they wouldn't for a bit but however eventually they did. We had a nice lot of traffic, what with corn and sugar beet and it varied according to the season. The corn was in sacks. Mr Raines, the farmer, used to bring it. There was no livestock or timber.

By 1927 Barton's passenger numbers were lower than any of the Ryedale stations. In that year 1357 tickets were bought – a daily average of about four and a half if Sundays are excluded. Even if the number is doubled, to allow for people coming to the village, nine per day was too few to sustain.

Above: Barton-le-Street station in early 1965, looking east. The second storey, added in 1863, can be identified. The NER promulgated a standard platform height of 2 ft 6 in in 1863, but, because of the low window sills in the main building, a higher extension had to be built. The wooden warehouse is beyond the platform frame. (Author)

Barton-le-Street's small goods yard from the top of the coal depot, also in early 1965. (Author)

Amotherby

Station masters

J. Smith	1853 - 1866
I. Harrison	1866 - 1879
I. Harrison (son)	1879 - 1881
John Robson	1881 - 1910
R.E. Andrew	1910 - 1926

supervised by Gilling from 1926
porter signalmen in charge

Jack Mitchell	(1943) - 1964

Station facilities: one two-level platform, five-cell coal depot, cattle dock, two small wooden warehouses, weighbridge and weigh office.

Amotherby's goods warehouse was small and timber-built and stood next to the road, opposite the station house. The lack of a proper warehouse was the subject of a letter from Thomas Parke of Newsham Mills only a few months after the line's opening. In 1862 Parke built his own private corn mill adjoining the station yard and the NER laid a siding to serve it. Parke's mill, as it was known throughout its railway life, was built of white bricks, with courses of red bricks at various levels, and a covered hoist at second floor level, over the siding. Another siding was added in 1861. The siding agreement was renewed in 1912 with Robert Rotherford Parke, in the same year that Frank Dawson went to work at Amotherby as a clerk:

It must have been quite a leisurely setup for the station master. On the passenger trains there was always plenty of room on most days. It was only special days that made a difference. Martinmas, in November, was hectic and the passenger trains were crammed. It was the one time in the year when the working people on the farms got a holiday. People went to the fair according to their district; all the villages between Gilling and Malton went to the Malton Martinmas fair.

In those days everything, absolutely everything, went by rail. When the pickup came there was always some traffic. We had the 'road wagon' for the small packages, which was a box wagon. To be unloaded into the wooden warehouse opposite the station house, the road wagon had to stand on the main line: the porter went inside with a wheelbarrow and unloaded the packages for our station. I used to do the checking of the invoices. There were also truck loads of agricultural feed - cattle cakes for different farmers, which the porter looked after.

There were two short sidings in the goods yard one of which also served the loading dock, and the other the coal depot. A long siding parallel to the main line could accommodate up 70 wagons. The layout was changed in later years to better suit the mill, which remained rail-served until the closure of the T&M in 1964. It was the existence of a contract with Parke's successors, the Brandsby Agricultural and Trading Association (BATA), that led to the Amotherby to Malton section of the T&M being closed ten weeks after the remainder.

Following the station's final closure in 1964 the building was razed and the empty space was used by the adjacent mill for parking and storage.

Below, upper: Amotherby station looking east. One of the station's small warehouses is on the left, the other on the right. (Lens of Sutton)
Below, lower: The pickup passing through Amotherby towards Gilling on 5 August 1964. Parke's mill is on the left. (Author)

7 - Stations (Gilling and Pickering)

The five G&P stations were in a more uniform style, not the least because all were built of stone. That the NER spent a good deal more on the five G&P stations is evident from their appearance but also from its records, which show that nearly £12,000 was spent on 'architectural works' by the contractor, Walker Stead. While some of this was spent on goods warehouses and lineside cottages, it contrasts with the £300 each - £2,100 in total - spent on the T&M's seven stations on its opening in 1853. Little wood was used for any of the buildings. They all possessed one feature which aided shunting: the line that led up onto the coal depot split into two and then converged before the depot was reached.

Nunnington

Station masters

W. Swales	1871 - 1874
Sharpe	1874 - 1884
R.W. Thornton	1884 -
John Robinson	(1890) - 1894
J. Groves	1894 - 1895
George Gray	1895 - 1909
Fred Gowland	1909 - 1917
John William Sellers	1917 - 1917
Fred Gowland	1917 - 1925

supervised by Helmsley from 1926
porters in charge

Tom Atkinson	1928 - 1953

public delivery siding from 1953

Station facilities: one platform, five-cell coal depot, cattle dock, two small timber warehouses, weighbridge and weigh office.

Nunnington station was situated on the hill down from Caukleys Bank into Ryedale, close to the road between Nunnington and Oswaldkirk. The building was a plain one, with heavy rock-faced stonework, T-shaped with a single-storey extension at the northern end, which contained the station office and waiting room. There were three living rooms and three bedrooms.

In earlier years Bob Hildreth was a carrier for Nunnington village; later he farmed nearby:

In those early years the station was pretty busy. The mail came there, and the papers; the postman went to the station for the letters. All the coal came there, which I used to lead. I delivered the produce, parcels and everything. After the First World War I led the War Memorial from a truck in the siding. It was all in one piece and it weighed between two and three tons. In the 1920s stone for the roads used to come to the station, blue stone, really sharp and hard. There were two places where we used to drop it: under a big oak tree on the road to Ness, and in Nunnington where there was a farm; there's a big copper beech tree there now. This old man, 'Boggy' Wilson, used to crack this stone into small pieces. There wasn't any welfare state then, it was either that or the workhouse.

Nunnington station from the south in the 1920s. (Arthur Cook/Author's Collection)

Nunnington during the winter, also in the 1920s. (Arthur Cook/Author's Collection)

(The stonebreaker used to be seen sitting on country lanes, beside a heap of stones 'tapping away from early morning until dewy eve, breaking up the large pieces of stone into pieces suitable for the kind of road repairing that preceded the tarmac era. He wore a shade over his eyes to protect him from flying splinters, and he worked steadily away, only pausing to exchange the time of day with an occasional passer-by…' – the *Yorkshire Gazette*, 3 January 1931.)

In 1926 the post of station master was dispensed with and Nunnington was placed under the control of Helmsley, with a porter in charge. From 1928 Tom Atkinson was the porter and he and his family lived there. His daughter, Rita Jackson, was born there and has vivid recollections of the station and life in the country:

It was a big draughty old house. There was the office and a waiting room. The waiting room was big and the office small. There was a Nestlés milk chocolate machine in the waiting room; Mr Naylor, the station master at Helmsley, came and emptied it once in a while. It was lovely chocolate, at a penny a bar. The railway telephone was in the office but the ordinary telephone was in the waiting room so that anyone could use it. Dad had his desk near the window, where he worked, and his telegraph instrument. There was another bell in the office. When he heard it Dad knew there was a train on its way. He used to go out and walk up and down the platform and wait for the train. After it had gone Dad came back in and he used to have to ring a bell to let the next station know that it was on its way. He had all his platform lamps to light, too.

We were self-sufficient: there was a field to go with the station and a very big yard. We had a big garden for vegetables and fruit, and Dad loved gardening. We had everything and Mum was always busy: ducks, geese, hens; goats for the milk and for making butter. A van used to come round and collect eggs; I think it was from Pickering. If Mum wanted some different chickens, she used to ring up Spinks of Easingwold in the afternoon and at night-time the chickens were on the train. After the last train had gone we used to walk down to the railway cottages at Cawton with our nanny goat. It wasn't far down the line. We used to leave it there for a day or two, and then we'd walk down and bring it back again. Mum was always hatching something!

The big houses at Nunnington and Laysthorpe used Nunnington station and, if they were having visitors and they wanted fish, they would ring York up and it was put on the train in the evening and the chauffeur would come down and collect it. As long as we kept to the lineside we were allowed to shoot and set snares for rabbits. Dad could fish under the Rye bridge too; that bit was railway land. He could fish elsewhere because he knew the farmers, but he could fish under the bridge without asking anyone. Dad used to get kindling for his fires, for the one in the office and the one in the waiting room. He used to ring York up and they used to send a wagon load of it. It was wagons they'd broken up, and all sorts of splinters and bits of wood. Dad had to chop them up. He also got so much coal, too.

The entrance to Nunnington goods yard. The change in gradient that gave problems to train crews shunting the yard, as decribed in Chpater 18, can be seen. (Author)

The father of Olive Russell, Fred Gowland, was Nunnington's station master from 1909 until 1925 and enjoyed the open air: 'he loved his gun. He had his terrier dog and had the privilege of going down the railway line to shoot rabbits. If any of the farmers were harvesting anywhere round about, my father was there when the rabbits used to run out. When they were getting to the end of a field with the binder, the rabbits used to start coming out and my father was there with his gun'.

In 1953, following the end of the passenger service and the retirement of Tom Atkinson, the station became a 'public delivery siding': open but without staff in attendance.

Helmsley

Station masters

Thomas Hesp	1871 - 1890
J. Dodd	1891 - 1891
W. Milsom	1891 - 1904
James Temple	1905 - 1925
Jim Terry	1925 - 1935
Harold Naylor	1935 - 1943
Ernest Leaman	1943 - 1953
Joe Hatfield	1953 - 1961
David Farr	1961 - 1964

Station facilities: two platforms, passing loop, signal box, eight-cell coal depot, carriage dock, cattle dock, goods warehouse, stable, weighbridge and weigh office.

In the nineteenth century Helmsley was dominated by the Earl of Feversham. In 1890 he owned the whole township, excepting three houses. In the 1865 agreement that saw the end of the LNYD, there was a clause that stipulated that: 'the North Eastern Company to provide at Helmsley a First Class station for passengers (including first and second class waiting rooms for ladies) with efficient accommodation for goods and timber and proper landing places for carriages &c. and Lord Feversham and his son the Honorable William Ernest Duncombe to be consulted as to the architecture and arrangements of such station'.

The result was that Helmsley station was unlike any other on the line. It was based on one of the standard designs of the NER Architect, Thomas Prosser, with a central two-storey section parallel to the platform, and single-storey cross wings projecting at each end, front and back. On the platform side the projections were carried forward by a long glazed verandah which provided shelter for waiting passengers; at the back the wings projected further, with another verandah between them. The station was built of sandstone but, unlike the other G&P stations, it was ashlar. The NER ensured that the detail of the station was in keeping with its aristocratic status, with decorations on the stonework. The cast iron supports for the glass verandah on the platform had Corinthian capitals and fluted lower halves. Station lighting was by gas from J. Smith's Helmsley gasworks from the day the station was opened in 1871. After many years' use, however, the gas pipes deteriorated to the extent that the supply became unreliable, but they remained in use until the end.

The Earl's influence over the design of the station extended even as far as the type of tiles or slates to be used for the roof. He wanted green Westmorland slates, instead of the blue Welsh slates which had been used at Nunnington and were the NER standard. A compromise was reached and green Westmorland slates were used, relieved by courses of purple slates of ornamental pattern. (Lord Feversham joined the NER Board in June 1872, to be succeeded by his son in 1879.)

A close-up of the roof of Helmsley station in 2004, showing the darker, scallop-edged Welsh slates against the Feversham-preferred Westmorland slates. This pattern is repeated over the entire roof. (Author)

Feversham got his five waiting rooms, a first and a second class each for ladies and gentlemen, and one for everyone else; there was a sixth of timber construction on the up platform. The five waiting rooms in the main building was an over-provision and four of them were later converted into two small two-roomed flats. The rest of the building was taken up by, downstairs, the station offices, together with kitchen, living room and sitting room for the station master and, upstairs, four large bedrooms and, later, a bathroom. Norman Race recalled Mrs Leaman, the wife of the station master Ernest Leaman, telling him that 'if ever she had any of the family ill in bed, by the time she got a meal to them it was cold. It was a route march to get to the far bedroom. The kitchen was right at the far end and you had to go along the passageway, past the sitting room and dining room, then up the terrific staircase. Mr Leaman used to say how many rolls of wallpaper he needed to paper the stairs: about 20 I think'.

The station yard was an extensive one, with five main sidings, one of which served the rather small stone-built warehouse. In 1912 another warehouse was built for the BATA. A later pre-fabricated concrete warehouse was used for the storage of animal feeding stuffs. The large side and end loading dock, used mostly by cattle, was to prove useful during the Second World War for tanks. From 1879 the delivery of goods was carried out by the NER and a one-horse stable was built in the yard. In later years, long after the introduction of motor vehicles, it was used for storage and at one time for calves belonging to the daughter of a station master, Joe Hatfield. In all, seven firms had timber businesses in the yard: including Joe Frank and Sons, Ben Frank and Sons, Hill Richard and Co. and the Yorkshire Pitwood Association; the Feversham Estate also had a very active sawmill.

Helmsley and Kirbymoorside were the long-time commercial hubs of the Railways of Ryedale. Helmsley handled more goods but Kirbymoorside had more passengers. In its heyday Helmsley employed five clerks, three of whom worked in a separate goods office near the weighbridge. When Roy Andrew went there as senior clerk in 1941: 'I found it a transformed place from the rather quiet place I remembered from previous visits. I had two lady clerks with experience, three inexperienced girls and a relief clerk, Gladys Potter. It was terrible to start with because you hadn't time to teach them'. These clerks were Mrs Ida D'Hooghe, Miss Temple, the daughter of a previous station master, Olive Wrightson (née Burn), Betty Watson (née Otterburn) and Rene Armstrong (née Armstrong) (Rene Armstrong married a man possessing the same surname as herself.) Olive Wrightson worked in both the passenger and the freight offices:

When I was on the early shift, I went before 7 a.m. for the passenger train and, after the morning passenger trains had gone, I went across to the goods office. When I was on the late shift I was in the ticket office, and finished after the last train at about 8pm, or later. We worked long hours, especially if there was a 'Red Alert' in York, when the evening train might be delayed and we might not get home until ten. Sometimes we'd be there for hours, just waiting for a train to come in. There were a lot of troops; we got them in batches going away and then there used to be those who were going away on leave, booking individually. We dealt with sacks too. I did sacks for most of my working life.

Rene Armstrong remembered Roy Andrew as 'a lovely man to work for. When I arrived the wartime business hadn't started, but when it did it became very, very busy.' There was a bell, or gong, on the signal box wall, which was rung by the signalman when a passenger train was about two minutes away. It had great resonance and drew passengers out of the waiting room. (There was a similar bell at Kirbymoorside.)

After the War ended Helmsley station became quieter. Muriel Rivis was a clerk from 1947 until the passenger service ended in early 1953: 'There were five clerks there at the start but latterly it was just Norman Race and me. Traffic was beginning to slow down but we had quite a few thousand tons of timber out of Duncombe Park. At the back end of summer there was a lot of potatoes and sugar beet. Farmers came down with tractors and trailers. They shovelled them in with the big forks that they used then'.

Norman Race was there from 1950 until 1956 and saw the end of the passenger service:

I started duty for the first train at about 7.20 a.m. and I got the delivery sheets for the parcels off that train done by a quarter to eight. I was in digs with a landlady in Pottergate, just outside the station yard, and I scarpered up there for my breakfast at about ten to eight, then back for the next train at about 8.20. I had about half an hour but if there were a lot of parcels it tended to cut down the breakfast. Once you got everything done and dusted and the second train went you went to the goods office. There was the 10.30 to York and the 11.45 back to Kirbymoorside. The evening one was at about half past six, with the return at about twenty to eight. Then the late morning train was withdrawn. The afternoon school train got in at about a quarter past four and waited until half past four. During the time at Helmsley, the driver would sometimes walk into the town for a packet of cigarettes. At this time coal was still in short supply and, while his back was turned, you could fill the coal bucket from the engine.

The town side of Helmsley station during the 1950s, showing the verandah that covered the space between the two projections of the main building. It can be seen that the building was asymmetrical, with an extension over the righthand projection which was probably erected as early as 1875.
(J.W. Armstrong Trust)

Helmsley station looking west some time before 1907, when a new signal box was opened. The fence behind the up, left, platform was emblazoned with enamel advertising signs. (Author's Collection)

Helmsley station in 1958 before the demolition of its glass verandah and after the passenger service had ceased, rendering the up platform redundant. The sheer size of the building, encompassing the five waiting rooms demanded by Lord Feversham, is obvious. (David Joy)

Under Helmsley's verandah during the 1950s. The ornate embellishments include Corinthian capitals and fluted lower halves to the cast iron columns, two 'serpent' seats - one behind the platform barrow - and a wall-mounted letter box. (J.W. Armstrong Trust)

In its heyday the Ministry of Food would buy up all the livestock that came into Helmsley market. They sent all the sheep away by rail. Sometimes we would have 80 wagons of livestock away, for two days in the week. They were mainly sheep, about 40 to a wagon, sometimes up to 3,000 or 4,000 in one day. However after the Ministry stopped buying the sheep it no longer automatically came to rail. Joe Hatfield had to go and canvas for it at the market. The only bargaining counter that he had for the rate was whether the wagon was to be charged at large, medium or small. There was a wooden partition that could be put into a cattle wagon; a large wagon could be made into a small one by putting this board in. So he could in effect charge the small price for a large load.

Collection and delivery in the country area was carried out for many years by Walter Caygill, until 1953 when he and his vehicle were moved to Malton. He covered a large area, covering Farndale, Bransdale, Bilsdale, Hawnby, Cold Kirby, Old Byland to the top of Sutton Bank, Gilling, Yearsley, Ampleforth and Nunnington. Mrs Caygill, his widow, recounted that:

Walter delivered all the parcels and goods that came in to the station. At one time he used to take loads of coal to the farms. In those days there was no coal delivery man to take coal in bags. It was all tipped out of a wagon at the station and Walter had it to shovel off at the other end. It was hard work. He used to deliver the Silcock's and Bibby's feeding stuffs, and general farm traffic. He delivered empty sacks and brought them back in full of grain. He took wines and spirits to pubs. He went to Arden Hall, Lord Mexborough's place, and to Murton Grange which was a big farm up Hawnby way belonging to Furness's, the shipping people. He used to go to Harpers above Skiplam; they were the people who showed sheep and won a lot of prizes.

Lady Marjorie Beckett, Lord Feversham's mother whose first husband was killed in the 1914-18 War, lived at Abbot's Well, Rievaulx, and every fortnight or so he used to deliver trees and shrubs for her garden. She had a beautiful garden. He was always invited in for a cup of tea. The housekeeper wasn't about so she made the tea and sat down and had a cup of tea with him. She was a very nice person.

One day during the War we lost him for a whole day! He went to work at half past seven and he hadn't come back at seven at night. Nobody knew where he was. He was taking a load of Silcock's to Murton Grange and the lorry broke down. He had to walk to Murton Grange to telephone for a mechanic to come out, and walk back to the lorry to make sure that no-one took any thing off it. He had to wait until someone came out and then deliver his load. It was half past seven at night when he got back.

Every Thursday was Farndale day. For Helmsley town itself there was a horse and rulley, with Lance Holmes. When they did away with that some time after the [Second] War, Walter delivered the town as well. He did the town in the morning and the villages in the afternoon. During the war, he used to deliver stuff to an Italian prisoner of war camp at Oswaldkirk. He once saw them boiling a great, big copper of spaghetti. He said that they were dropping half pounds of margarine into it and it didn't look very nice at all! After the line closed to passengers in 1953 we moved to Malton. He used to load up with passenger parcels at Malton and with goods at Helmsley.

When the station was opened in 1871 it had an engine shed. The engine hauled the first train to, and the last train from, Gilling each day. When the section to Kirbymoorside was opened in 1874 the shed became redundant and was removed. The wording of the NER minute that records the removal suggests that it may have been of wooden construction.

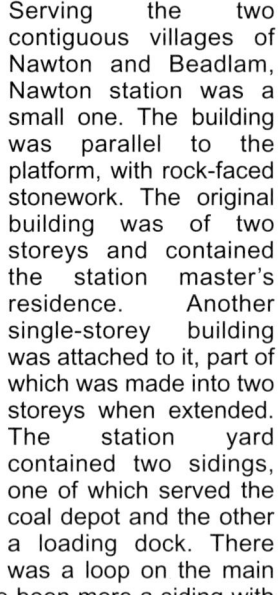

Nawton station, probably shortly after opening and certainly before 1883 when the building was enlarged at the request of the station master, Thomas Wainwright. (Author's Collection)

Nawton
Station masters
Thomas Wainwright	1874 - 1889
William Wainwright	1890 - 1918
J. Cherrington	1918 - 1927
E.B. Mowforth	1927 - 1932

supervised by Kirbymoorside from 1932
porters in charge
Smith	- 1941
Ronald Vivian Vincent Lee	1941 - 1964

Station facilities: one platform, five-cell coal depot, carriage dock, cattle dock, goods warehouse, weighbridge and weigh office.

Nawton station looking east after 1883, with the staff cottages on the right. (Author's Collection)

Serving the two contiguous villages of Nawton and Beadlam, Nawton station was a small one. The building was parallel to the platform, with rock-faced stonework. The original building was of two storeys and contained the station master's residence. Another single-storey building was attached to it, part of which was made into two storeys when extended. The station yard contained two sidings, one of which served the coal depot and the other a loading dock. There was a loop on the main line, but this seems to have been more a siding with a connection at each end. The connection at the Kirbymoorside end of the loop was later removed.

In 1932 Nawton station was placed under the control of Kirbymoorside with a porter in charge. Ron Lee was the porter from 1941 until the station closed in 1964. (His son Desmond also worked on the G&P, being the last porter signalman at Helmsley.) Ron Lee was known as a very conscientious worker. He worked in the office during the proper hours and then went into the house for meals. But he was always willing to return out of hours if he was required.

For a time Nawton had a strong connection with food. In the 1920s there was a considerable traffic in soft fruit. Ernest Leaman: 'it was a busy little place in the season. All around there was a lot of fruit, especially plums. On one occasion we had practically the whole length of the platform filled with baskets of plums, waiting for the train to come in'.

Arthur Cook remembered that 'in the fruit time it used to take a quarter of an hour to load the evening train to York with the fruit. There were bags and bags of gooseberries and things like that'. During the Second War a buffer depot was built behind the station, with its own siding. It was used to store all manner of food: dried eggs and fruit, sugar, corned beef. There was a continuous traffic to and from the warehouse. After the War raw sugar was brought in special trains for storage there. 11,000 quarters of barley were stored in a hangar at Wombleton airfield. All these products eventually went away by rail, bringing an unusual amount of activity to what had become a very quiet station. Don Watson, then a porter at Kirbymoorside, worked there: 'I used to finish at Kirbymoorside on a Saturday dinnertime, go to the food dump on a Saturday afternoon and Sunday morning, and work there, loading stuff on the railway but for the Ministry as a casual labourer'.

Betty Watson was at the station, the last full-time clerk there, from 1943 until 1947:

My first introduction to Nawton station was arriving there at about ten to nine. There was another relief porter there called Reg Hepton. I walked into the office and there were five mice in one trap. They were absolutely overrun with mice, I think because of that food store. I refused to work in that office until they got it cleaned up. I used to dash in, get what books I wanted and go into the waiting room. Had I but known, they were just as rife in the waiting room as in the office!

A view of Nawton station from the rear of a brake van of a Kirbymoorside-bound pickup in June 1964. Despite the lack of regular passenger trains for 11 years a platform barrow remains ready for use. (Tom Walker)

There was a garden at the end of the station building nearest the level crossing. It had been allowed to go to ruin. Ron Lee, Reg Hepton and I set to and tidied it up. It was a lovely little garden and in the middle there was a fountain. We never did get the fountain working again, but at least we unearthed it from the wilderness and we got the garden looking nice again. Blue tits used to nest there.

Doreen Wilson was the daughter of Ron Lee and lived in the station house:

My Dad was the porter in charge of Nawton from 1941 until the station closed in 1964. Everybody who came to the station used to call him the station master. He never had any time off, as the farmers came in with their grain and different things, or there was the coal: there was always someone after him. He worked in the office during the proper hours and then come in to the house for meals. But he was on the job all the time and he was always jumping up and we would say 'let them wait' but he wouldn't. My Dad was a good worker and Mr Dobson, the station master at Kirbymoorside, realised this and that, left alone, Dad would get on with the job.

The two-storey part of the house was the domestic side and the one-storey part the railway part. The front door was at the back. Downstairs there were the sitting room and living room; the scullery and kitchen were at the back, below the bathroom. A wall enclosed a little back yard with a couple of little rooms, a toilet and a little shed. The

stairs went up the middle and a long corridor went along the back, upstairs. There were three bedrooms upstairs, and the bathroom. The bathroom was a later addition, as it stuck out from the rest of the house and was rendered or pebble-dashed. There was no electricity. There was cold water and an old Yorkist range to heat it and do the cooking. When we arrived we filled a two pound jam jar full of nails which had been hammered into the walls. They had kept coal in the bath!

Kirbymoorside
Station masters

Richard Jennings	1873 - (1897)
T.P. Tilly	1901 - 1912
J.T. Forster	1912 - 1926
J. G. Wilson	1926 - 1932
Jabez Alfred Davies	1932 - 1942
James Herbert Dobson	1942 - 1955
Stuart Hunsley	1955 - 1956
E. Gordon Triffitt	1956 - 1957
Don F.C. Baker	1957 - 1958
Ted Letby	1958 - 1961
Jack Dugdale	1961 - 1964

Station facilities: two platforms, passing loop, signal box, yard crane, eight-cell coal depot, carriage dock, cattle dock, goods warehouse, weighbridge and weigh office.

The station was at the foot of Piercy End (which was renamed Railway Street), and about 400 yards from the town's Market Place. With the exception of the livestock loading dock, all the station's facilities lay on the north side of the line. It consisted of an L-shaped two-storey house, which was the station master's residence, and a projecting T-shaped single-storey wing for the station offices. The space over the platform between the wings was spanned by a glazed verandah. The stonework was rough-hewn, familiar from the other G&P stations, Helmsley excepted. Passengers intending to make a journey came through a door from the station yard into the waiting room-cum-booking hall, which had seats around the walls. The booking office window was on the right and a door straight ahead led out onto the platform. There was also another small waiting room for ladies, seldom used in later years other than for storage. There was also a timber-built waiting room on the up platform.

Initially four sidings were provided, one of which served the temporary engine shed that remained until the line through to Pickering was opened in 1875. In 1876 two more sidings were installed, specifically for loading timber. A 3-ton derrick was set up adjacent to the timber sidings in 1877. The stone-built goods warehouse was served by a siding which passed through the building. When the station was first opened it was equipped with a 5-ton weighbridge, which was replaced in 1934 by one of

An early view of Kirbymoorside (when it was spelled with a - between 'Kirby' and 'Moorside') and the station staff and the station master's wife. The full extent of the fine building is well portrayed in this and the following photograph. (Author's Collection)

20 tons. In the same year 124 square yards of land at the goods yard entrance were sold to the North Riding County Council for £10, to enable the present roundabout to be made.

Livestock was important at Kirbymoorside until the traffic ceased in August 1952. Between 1885 and 1907 between 4000 and 5000 wagons of livestock were handled each year. The speciality at Kirbymoorside was sheep, and during and after the Second World War the Ministry of Food despatched considerable numbers from the station. Sometimes two or three special trains were run. Harry Young was a porter signalman at the station from 1940 until 1958: 'the animals were loaded while the engine was waiting. The cattle dock held 13 wagons so we would put the 13 in, load them up, get the engine to take them out and put them in another siding, then put another 13 wagons in, as they were wanted. A 45-wagon train would take practically a whole day'. Percy Perrin, a livestock loader, came out from Malton:

The busiest time was from February into June when I went to Kirbymoorside every week. We had quite a few Moorjocks: small sheep that could be loaded up to 50 or 60 in a wagon; more if they were clipped. The Rannochs were bigger. We used to load 30 wool sheep into a wagon or up to 50 clipped ones. They weren't pinched for room but they would keep warm. We had quite a few casualties when they were shunting. They used to shunt them very hard sometimes and they all went to one end. When one went down it couldn't get up.

Mostly the animals were walked down to the station from the market. It was a bit tricky loading: there were one or two awkward openings on the way down to the station where they could slip away down. There was many a time when they missed the entrance into the dock and we had to run down the road after them.

Several commodities were sent out from specialist Kirbymoorside manufacturers: pigeon clocks from Boddy's, pigeon lofts from Porritt's, wire from Harvest Saver and Implement, bracken breakers from Colonel Holt, farm machinery from Russell's, and gliders from Slingsby Sailplanes. The pigeon clocks were sent by William Eanus Boddy, a watchmaker and jeweller with an interest in pigeons and who had bought several hundreds clocks at a 'job lot' price and leased them for £2 or £3 a season. They all went by train. Richard Boddy, his nephew and a clerk at the station from 1951 to 1954, remembered the parcels office floor being lined with pigeon clocks. Porritt's pigeon lofts, National Sectional Buildings, originated from a family firm with

Another early view of Kirbymoorside station. The booking office is behind the bay-fronted window. The bearded man second from right, also to be seen in the previous photograph, is Richard Jennings, the first station master. (Author's Collection)

a life-long interest in pigeon racing, which started building pigeon lofts in 1907 and gained a reputation for high quality. The pigeon lofts went all over the country, including to the Shetland Islands and to the Royal Air Force.

Harvest Saver and Implement was initially an independent company in Kirbymoorside which manufactured plain wire and barbed wire, electric fencing. Colonel Vernon Holt of Ravenswick, near Kirbymoorside, was an innovator in farm machinery and developed a machine that recovered land that had fallen to the spread of bracken. The bracken breaker consisted of a heavy metal bar pivoted at both ends in a frame designed to be drawn by a horse or, later, a tractor. According to Derek Hey, a clerk at the station in 1947 and 1948: 'the machines were very heavy, with toothed rotating arms. They were in different sizes. We sent quite a lot away from Kirbymoorside'. Colonel Holt's bracken breakers pale into insignificance against Russell's implements. Ted Letby, Kirbymoorside's station master from 1958 to 1961: 'we could send as many as nine or ten implements away in a day. We used to put them on 'lowfits' and strap them down, which was quite an art, but the porters had it off and made a very good job of it'.

Slingsby Sailplanes had started in the 1930s, making gliders in a part of Russell's works. At the beginning of the Second World War they became independent. The gliders were in sections packed in long crates and were fitted together at the destination. Keith Cass, a clerk at Kirbymoorside from 1950 to 1956, remembered that they were 'big things but they were packed into beautifully-made crates. We used to get LMS 'long lows' for these crates and they would look lost on them, as these wagons were so long. I've seen three of these long lows in a rake in the yard. We had one or two gliders for King Farouk of Egypt'.

A view of Kirbymoorside station and its goods yard looking west in July 1964. The goods shed is to the right of the slope up on to the coal depot, and outside it are several permanently-parked box wagons for animal feeding stuffs. The yard crane is to their right. (Author)

Soft fruit went out in season. Plums came from Marser Ellerker who kept a large orchard near Keldholme and used local child labour to pick the fruit, which included gooseberries growing between the plum trees. His plums are especially remembered by Keith Cass in a way that might not be expected: 'he came down to the station, saying that he had seven hundredweight of plums, say. We knew full well that he had a bit more. But it wasn't as daft as it sounded, because the first thing that you did after he had gone was to lift up the corner and take a plum out. The porter did the same, and the guard on the train did, and the porters at York. So, by the time they arrived at the destination, there were about seven hundredweight'.

In Kirbymoorside town the collection and delivery was entrusted to Frank Clark, and later his son Jim, of whom many a tale has been told, some of which are in Chapter 20. Collection and delivery in the country area was carried out for many years by Bob Atkinson, then later Bob Alderton who drove out from Malton each morning.

Through all the years of its existence Kirbymoorside station annually sold more passenger tickets than any other station on the T&M and G&P. Inasmuch as the town was the largest centre of population in the Ryedale area (Pickering and Malton excepted) this is not surprising. The office at Kirbymoorside was the standard pattern between the platform and the yard, with bay windows at both ends. Betty Woodhouse (née Armstrong) was a clerk there from 1943: 'along the side wall there was a fixture in which all the books were kept: the account book, charging scales and everything else. There were oil lamps in the office and we had to strain our eyes to see. The coal bucket used to stand by the fire. We never had enough coal and we used to go out to the engine driver with a bucket to get a bit'.

There was a step up to the ticket window. The tickets were held in 'tubes' at the side and the ticket date punch was to the right of the window. In front of the window there was a high desk with drawers, the top one for the cash with three 'scoops' for coins. On selling a ticket the clerk slipped it out from the bottom of its tube. Longer-term stocks of tickets were kept in drawers below the desk, each of which held thousands of tickets. When Keith Cass arrived there he found that 'the top three or four drawers had stock in; then there were three empty drawers and two at the bottom which wouldn't open. You could get at the one second to the bottom by pulling the one above it right out but not the bottom one. So once, when I was on the late shift, and there wasn't much doing I used the poker to get it open. It was full of tickets, several thousands of them. I checked the ticket

registers, including old ones that were kept in the muniment room, which was the old waiting room on the other platform, and there was no record of them'. The tickets were new from when the station had first been opened in 1874, and had lain undisturbed for nearly 80 years. On the instructions of the auditors the tickets were destroyed, but only after some had been kept by the clerks at the station (and some sent to the Railway Museum in York).

Keith Cass has told a story about one of his Kirbymoorside customers and this book would be incomplete without it: 'we had a delightful old gentleman who came to the station about twice a week. He would present himself at the window and ask for a return: "Yes, but where are you going?" I said. "Give me a return, and none of your lip." "Yes, but I need to know where you want it to." "If I tell you it'll be all over the town." So we gave him one to York and he would rebook there'.

Sinnington

Station masters

E. Lobatto	1875 - 1875
T. Geldart	1875 -
John William Dixon	(1897) - 1899
G.W. Horner	1899 - 1917
Fred Gowland	1917
John William Sellers	1917 - 1933
T.J. Ruston	1933 - 1936
John Robert Sleight	1936 - 1938
R. William Harwood	1938 - 1940
Fred Newlove	1940 - 1944
W.A. Arnett	1944 - 1952
Bernard Artley *	1952 - 1953

* relief station master

Station facilities: one platform, five-cell coal depot, horse dock, cattle dock, timber goods warehouse, weighbridge and weigh office.

Sinnington was the last of the thirteen stations on the combined T&M and G&P to be opened, in 1875, and the first to be completely closed, in 1953. There was a single platform on the down side of the line. The building was similar to that of Kirbymoorside: two storeys for the station master's living accommodation and a single storey for the station offices. There was an office, and a general waiting room and a ladies waiting room. Three sidings served the goods yard: one to the coal depot. Another siding ran alongside the main line and ended at the livestock loading dock adjacent to the road to Marton. Frank Pickett started his railway career there in March 1924, until 1926 when he went Grosmont:

The station master was John William Sellers and he was a good station master as long as you did your work. He had a big moustache and, when he came out in the morning, if the moustache was stood out horizontally, you had to look out! Sinnington was a busy station then; we were hard at it all day long, handling hay, straw, grain and potatoes. Hay was loaded, sheeted and roped on double bolsters. These were strange wagons to use and you had to know what you were doing. We used an even stranger wagon for hay when wagons were in short supply: a hopper.

Sinnington station in about 1900 looking east. The station's strong similarity to Kirbymoorside is obvious. The people on the only platform appear to be waiting for a train. (Author's Collection)

There was stuff for Sinnington Mill about a mile from the station, nearly at Marton, down in the 'Low Country': cotton cake, linseed cake, maize - everything that a mill sells came in by rail, which Turnbull's led to the Mill. The cotton cake and linseed cake came from the B.O.C.M. places at Selby and Liverpool; the maize probably came from abroad. We had quite a bit of sack business with the mill. The Mill also milled their own stuff: barley and wheat. Mr Daniel Turnbull himself used to go by train every Tuesday to Leeds corn market. In those days he had a pony and trap and he used to drive up to the station to go on the early train from Sinnington.

Both the other porter and I played football for the village. On Saturday afternoon, if we got our work done, Mr Sellers let us both go to play football. We would maybe load five double bolsters of hay ready for the pickup in the afternoon. Mr Sellers used to pay the ganger of the length, I think it was a shilling, to open the gates, and tranship the goods from the road wagon - our job - so that we could play football in the afternoon.

I played cricket too. The cricket and football field, and a tennis court, were just over the railings from the station. As they were practising I went over and did a bit of fielding and a bit of batting between trains. Then I played for them regularly.

John Lumley was the local carter for many years. He had a horse and rulley and delivered mainly to Marton, but also to Normanby:

My Dad died when I was only $13\frac{1}{2}$ and I had to leave school and take over. The station master had the coal sale and I used to buy coal from him. In those days coal went by the name of the colliery and not in grades. The best coal that came to Sinnington when I was leading it was Whitwood and cost £2 a ton. The second grade was about £1 10s a ton; it's a lot of difference. There were a few people who bought Whitwood. I bagged the coal and I used to lead it down to Marton at 3d a bag which was a hundredweight. That was all I got out of it. Later I went up to 4d and up to 6d before we finished. I would lead it loose if I could get it up to someone's coal house and shove it straight in through a window in the wall. I finished leading coal when the station closed in 1953.

At one time I did lead up to Sinnington village and I was paid by the railway to do it. There was an old lady living at Sinnington Hall called Miss Kendal. I used to lead to her a grocery box every month from Harrods. The shop in Sinnington used to get a lot of wholesale stuff, buns and confectionery; they would get maybe half a dozen boxes.

In common with elsewhere, passenger use of the station declined very severely through the 1920s and 1930s. During the 1930s around 1750 passenger tickets were sold per annum – barely 35 per week. Although the station was near to Sinnington, buses went into the village and provided a more frequent service.

Reg Sleightholme was a clerk in late 1936: 'one thing we did made the news as it was rather unusual: a farm removal. It was quite an event at the time. A local farmer at Marton moved to Hawsker, near Whitby, complete. There would be about 20 to 30 wagons: all his stock, implements: the lot. It was a complete special train all to himself. There was a coach for him and his family'.

One of the most fondly remembered station masters was the last full-time one, W.A. Arnett. He was known as a genial man, with 11 or 12 children, and the proud owner of a 1931 Rolls Royce. Betty Woodhouse remembered him as 'a very genial fellow: he always had smile and a wave and he was a very good-hearted person'. It was said that he used this vehicle to deliver coal, but many people remembered the joy of being given a lift. Arnett and his large family emigrated to Australia a few months before the station was closed. Bernard Artley, a relief station master, served the station for its remaining life before it was closed at the beginning of 1953:

It wasn't a busy station. There was a bit of grain from farmers going away to stores. There was the coal sale, which I took over for the last five months. I remember the last day of the service well because it was the day of the East Coast floods. It was a terrible day because that afternoon a chimney blew off the station house and came through the glass verandah and into the office door. I was in the office at the time but there was nobody about. When the station closed I stayed on for about a week to clear up. I had a list of outstandings; I went round and eventually I collected them.

Sinnington station on the very last day of its service to the local area, 31 January 1953. Note that the siding is resting on a mix of concrete blocks and conventional sleepers. (J.W. Armstrong Trust)

8 - Sidings

Angram siding

In April 1880 Mr Frank, timber merchant of Helmsley, was in the process of cutting down Angram Wood, about 600 yards north east of Husthwaite Gate station on the T&M. He sought the NER's permission to connect a tramway from Angram Wood to the station siding. The NER agreed on condition that the work was carried out to the satisfaction of the company's engineer and at Frank's expense, and that he arranged with the local authority for permission to cross the road by the station. The tramway must have been about a third of a mile in length. It may have been narrow gauge and it is likely to have existed for a few weeks at most.

Pye Pits siding

The report of the Board of Trade Inspector into the T&M when it was opened in 1853 referred to a siding at the 'Malton Pie-pits'. It was on an incline and may have been between the two bridges over the T&M in Old Malton, where there was a limestone quarry. In 1856 the NER and the Malton and North Grimston Limestone Company signed an agreement for a siding into the latter's quarry in Old Malton. This in turn became known as Pye Pits siding and was a quarter of a mile from the original Pie Pits, and three quarters of a mile from Scarborough Road junction. It was worked by a five-lever ground frame.

From its junction with the T&M, the Pye Pits siding climbed alongside Pasture Lane and under a bridge under Peasey Hills Road into the quarry. The quarry was some 40 feet deep, with sheer walls; railings protected passers by from falling over the edge. Paul Jackson lived with his family close to the T&M and, for them and for others, the Pye Pits lime kilns had their own special attraction: 'when we children were young and when winter was coming on our mother would take us to Pye Pits, there to hang over the edge of the sheer drop above the lime kilns, to inhale the pungent smoke. The idea was that it would keep the colds away. It was common for people to do this. I don't know if it ever did us any good but it smelled as if it must have done!'

In the early years some stone, how much is not known, was conveyed by rail only as far as Malton, to the River Derwent Navigation, where it was loaded into barges. Lime was also conveyed to stations along the T&M to farmers' fields. Part of the siding also later served a Council depot where roadstone was received by rail and shovelled through openings in the walls of an adjacent building, to be piled on the floor. The siding agreement was terminated in May 1931. The date of the quarry's closure is not known but it is said to have become inevitable after a lump of stone was thrown by a blast through the window of a nearby house.

In August 1872 the Yorkshire Agricultural Society held its annual show in Malton, on a large cowpasture on the side of the Outgang Road near Pasture Lane gatehouse, about half a mile from Pye Pits. The *Yorkshire Gazette* records the contribution made by the T&M: 'the railway arrangements were in every way satisfactory. The North Eastern Railway Company constructed a siding from the Malton and Thirsk line on the ground near the traction ring. The

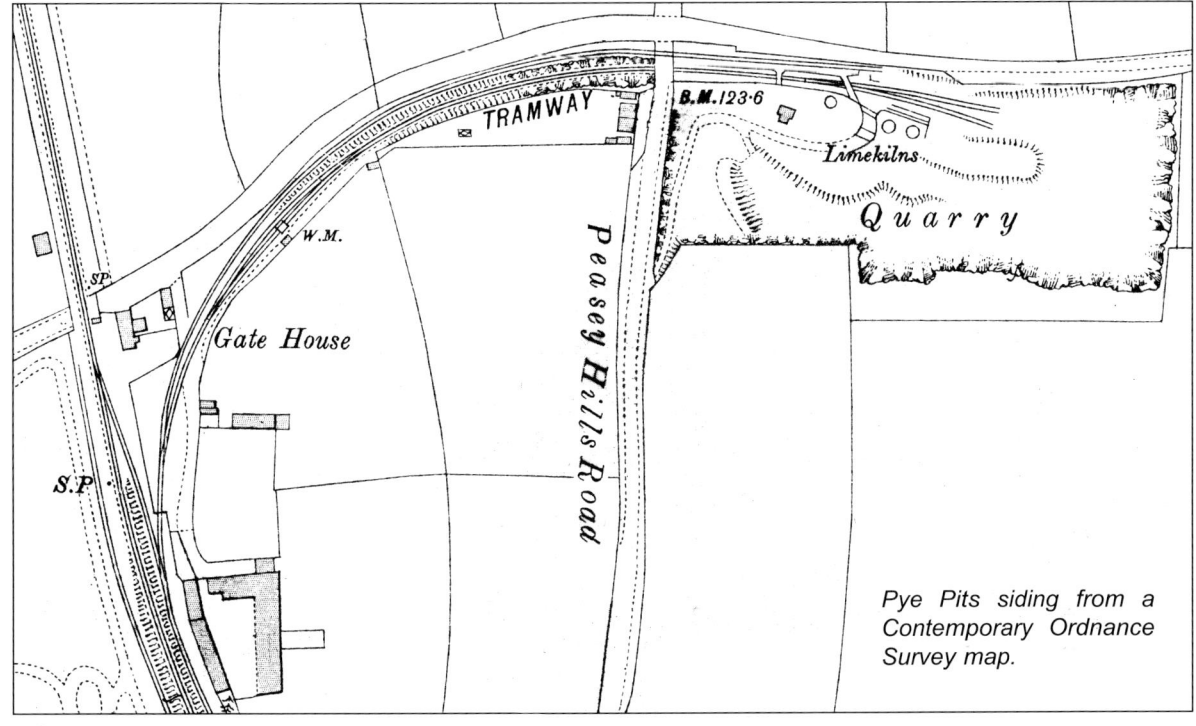

Pye Pits siding from a Contemporary Ordnance Survey map.

siding had three lines of rails and it was of immense advantage in landing stock and implements'.

In 1904 electricity cables were laid along the side of the T&M from the Northern Counties Supply Co's power station near Pye Pits to Norton. The cables were buried in a wooden duct filled with compound and covered with tiles; they fell out of use in the mid 1920s. In 1955, owing to the rising value of copper, parts were recovered between Pye Pits and the Old Malton road bridge. A BR locomotive and crew were hired for the day, with platelayers to reinstate the track side. The cables were cut into 20-yard lengths and two unsuccessful attempts were made pull these out of the duct. When the cable was doubled back on itself 20 yard lengths were recovered rapidly and by late afternoon lengths up to 150 yards had been brought out. In all 600 yards were recovered during the day, weighing about $4\frac{1}{2}$ tons, which were loaded on to an empty truck attached to the engine.

Harome siding

Although the local people requested one, the village of Harome never had its own station. Instead it had a 41 yard siding, three quarters of a mile from the village, and $1\frac{1}{4}$ miles from Nunnington station. The NER did at least pave the way for a possible station, however. One of the two buildings that was provided for the railway workers (see Chapter 15) was adjacent to the line, and its ground floor was several feet higher than that of the other house. It could have been converted into a station and a platform could have been provided without the building having to be altered.

The opening of the siding caused some ructions within the NER. Lieutenant-Colonel J.H. Rich of the Board of Trade inspected it in November 1872 and was not pleased with what he found: 'the locking of the catch points is defective and allows the signals to be lowered when the points are open to allow vehicles to come out of the sidings... It appeared that neither the Engineer of the North Eastern Railway, the District Engineer or the Assistant to the District Engineer had inspected it before I went there. Under such management it cannot be wondered at, that the North Eastern Railway Company were distinguished last year and stood second on the list for the record of accidents'.

The NER management was incensed by the criticism. The Secretary, C.S. Wilkinson, replied, stating that the Directors had expressed 'their confident belief that the regulations of the Board of Trade do not sanction the tone of general censure by their Inspecting Officers when reporting on matters of a special character'. The Board of Trade replied, stating that Colonel Rich had 'found that … the man in charge could shift the points for any vehicle to run from the siding on to the passenger line while the signals were lowered for passenger trains to pass... [He] was informed that none of the Engineers of the Co. had visited the works before he went there'. The NER was in the wrong and an instruction was given that before submitting new works to an inspection by the Board of Trade, they should be properly inspected and approved by the company's officers. Harome siding was formally inspected again and opened in December 1873.

The siding held up to five wagons and was a public delivery siding. There was also a level crossing there, complete with crossing keeper but, as the road only led to fields, there was little for the latter to do. The gates were kept open for the trains and only rarely did they need to be closed for a vehicle. It was worked by a six-lever ground frame.

Latterly Harome siding was quiet for most of the time. Archie Greenley, who lived in one of the nearby cottages, noted that 'coal was led by an ex-army man and another chap, a ton at a time with a horse and cart, who had to shovel it out of the wagon'. Lime came from ICI for spreading on the nearby fields, but the main traffic in later years was sugar beet, when it was very busy for a short time in the autumn of each year. George Jackson: 'it was the Wasses from Wombleton Grange that used Harome siding, and one or two in Harome itself. They used to put sugar beet on there'. The siding was used for the first time for many years when the track was taken up following closure in 1964.

Harome siding in 1964, looking south towards Nunnington. (Author)

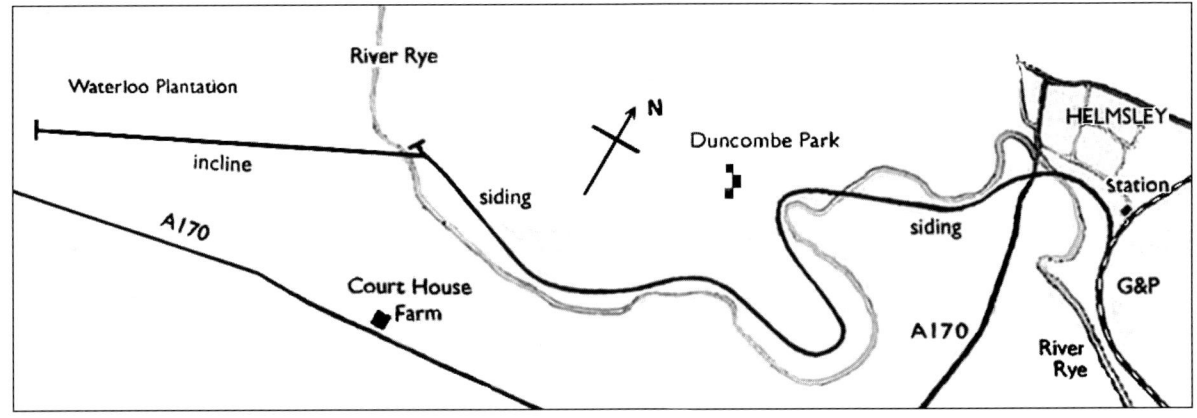

The Duncombe park siding wound its way up the valley of the River Rye for about 2½ miles to the foot of a steep incline up into Waterloo Plantation.

Duncombe Park siding, Helmsley

In 1918, during the First World War, a siding was laid into the Feversham Estate for the extraction of timber from Waterloo Plantation. It commenced in the station yard, crossed the River Rye and the A170 road, and wound its way for two and a half miles up the valley, crossing the river two further times before reaching the foot of an incline. The incline itself was almost a mile in length.

The agreement between the NER and the Yorkshire Pitwood Association Ltd. (YPA) in March 1918 included the provision of three sidings on the edge of the NER's Helmsley goods yard, each of which held up to 20 wagons. The YPA undertook to pay the wages of two men employed by the NER to 'supervise the loading at the actual forwarding point and to pass the loads at the exchange sidings'. In other words, these men were there to ensure that the loads were properly secured and within the railway loading gauge.

Three timber exchange sidings were installed on the edge of Helmsley station, where the residential street Southlands is now to be found. Timber is seen here waiting to be dispatched, each load occupying several wagons. (Charles Allenby Collection)

The foot of the incline up to Waterloo Plantation. A line of wagons can be seen in the left background, as well as in the spur bottom left. (Charles Allenby Collection)

The London firm of Hill Richard and Company, Contractor for Public Works, had the siding for a while, but in 1921 it was taken over by the Feversham family. Some 40,000 tons of timber passed through the station in the four years from 1918. NER locomotives did not venture beyond Helmsley station yard and no information has come down as to the motive power used within the Feversham Estate.

The head of the Waterloo Plantation incline. The military caps worn by two of the men suggest that the photograph was taken during the First World War. (Charles Allenby Collection)

The siding agreement was formally terminated in 1935. Traces remain, including the route of the incline, much overgrown but visible when the present trees are leafless. Several level places along the valley floor are visible to those who look for them.

Spaunton Quarry

In the late 1920s George Hodsman and Sons (1928) Ltd. opened a limestone quarry on Spaunton Moor, on the south edge of the North York Moors. In October 1930 the LNER laid a siding into the quarry from a point about 300 yards east of Catter Beck level crossing, half way between Kirbymoorside and Sinnington stations. From the junction with the G&P the siding curved round to and crossed Catter Beck and the A170 road. Once across the road, the siding climbed steeply into the quarry.

The siding was shunted by the locomotives of Pickering-bound goods trains, which backed into the quarry, pushing empties up to the highest point. When required for loading their brakes were released and they were allowed to run down to the stone hoppers for loading. Loaded wagons were removed by the same train and taken on to Pickering. During the Second World War the quarry was busy and wagons were brought out on most days. There are no railway records of the tonnage forwarded from the quarry but it is likely that upwards of 12,000 tons annually were despatched in the early years. Later, however, there was a severe decline. Some of the stone was used as railway ballast but perhaps even more for road surfaces. For this purpose tanks of tar were sent to the quarry by rail, reheated on arrival and mixed with stone, ready for surfacing the roads. Earlier, the wagons of stone had been taken into Pickering and on to Grosmont where Hodsman had a tarmacadam plant.

The siding was maintained by LNER staff, including platelayer Tom Magson: 'we used to repair the track into the quarry for them if there were any sleepers that needed replacing. The sleepers used to get rotten and they just used to part. It got bad at the finish: we had an engine off two or three times. The loco used to drop down and that was it'. In February 1948 a locomotive was derailed, coming to rest with all its wheels on the ground. The quarry siding was not used again.

Other agreements

Perhaps the strangest agreement was that between the NER and Messrs Beckett and Co., bankers of York, in May 1909. The agreement permitted Beckett's representatives to carry loaded revolvers 'when travelling in charge of specie' – carrying cash – on nominated trains. As far as the Ryedale lines were concerned Beckett's staff used the 11.34 a.m. train from Helmsley to Kirbymoorside, with return at 3.32 p.m. or 5.54 p.m., every day except Fridays; and from Malton to Kirbymoorside at 10.10 a.m. and return at 3.32 p.m. or 5.54 p.m. '5 or 6 annually'. The termination of this agreement is not recorded.

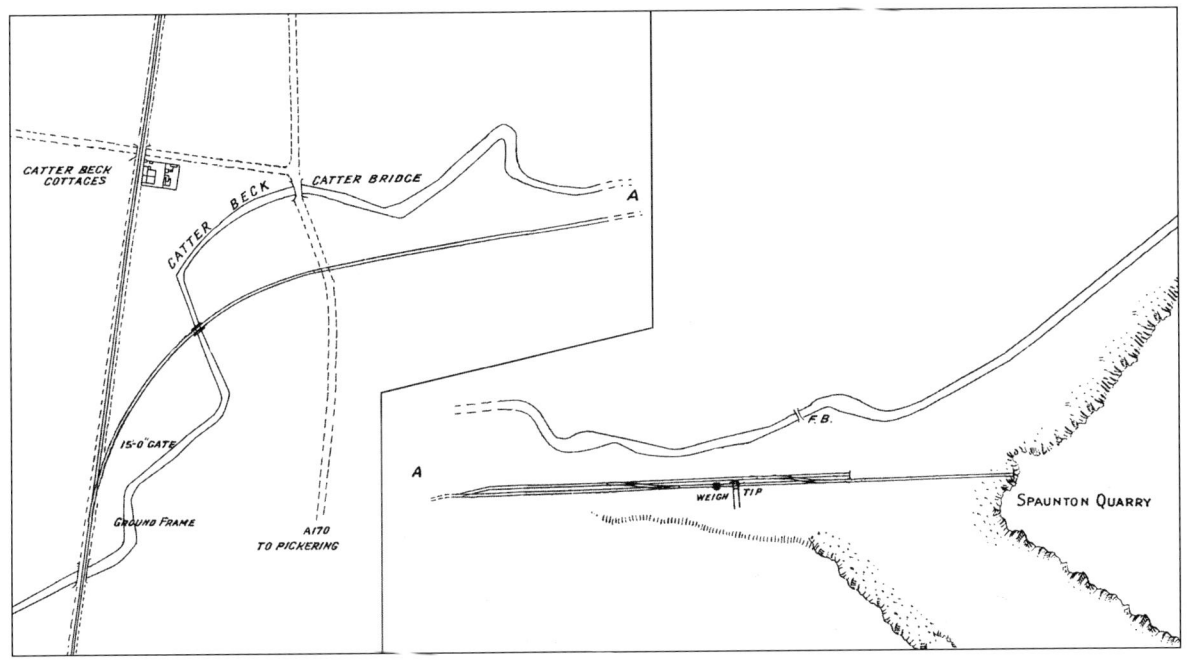

Spaunton Quarry siding from the map that accompanied the formal agreement between the LNER and George Hodsman and Sons in 1930.

9 - Heyday and Decline

D49 Hunt Class 4-4-0 No 62736 The Bramham Moor on a Pickering to York train, about to round the Raskelf Curve from Sunbeck junction to the main line at Bishophouse junction, on 29 July 1949. The north curve can be discerned behind the front of the engine. (Ken Hoole Collection)

Following their completion in 1875 the Railways of Ryedale fulfilled their function of serving the local populations. The variations in the timetables and changes in methods of signalling and track maintenance are described in other chapters. 1870 saw the original 46-span timber bridge over the River Derwent at Malton replaced by a three-span girder bridge and an extended embankment. The other original timber underbridges were nearly all replaced by the 1920s. Following very serious floods in 1878 and again in 1880, the York to Scarborough line in Norton was raised in 1881, which necessitated raising the T&M's bridge over that line and made the initial climb from Scarborough Road much steeper.

In the years before the First World War the conveyance of goods and passengers by road was still mostly dependent on the horse but it was growing, albeit slowly. There was a small decline in rail traffic in the first decade of the century. That War saw the production of motor vehicles on a huge scale, mostly for the carriage of war matériel. After its end much of this was sold and instigated a rapid development of road transport for both goods and passengers.

The tables below give data firstly for goods and then for passenger traffic at each of the thirteen stations in the years 1885, 1904, 1914, 1920, 1927, 1934 and 1938:

Goods tonnage forwarded								
Station	1885	1904	1914	1920	1927	change 1904-27	1934	1938
Husthwaite Gate	665	1314	1323	1078	1084	-17.5%	1297	556
Coxwold	1095	1199	871	1415	1587	+32.3%	844	723
Ampleforth	705	978	1053	489	836	-14.5%	252	241
Gilling	1890	1882	1835	1915	2532	+34.5%	6615	5900
Hovingham Spa	1400	1697	1676	2243	1219	-28.2%	*	*
Slingsby	667	869	1245	1292	932	+7.2%	*	*
Barton-le-Street	422	562	805	765	811	+44.3%	*	*
Amotherby	2049	2326	1470	2126	1050	-54.9%	*	*
Nunnington	647	921	1004	812	744	-19.2%	772	385
Helmsley	4292	4360	4776	11,060	6129	+40.6%	10,596	12,313
Nawton	605	888	782	542	570	-35.8%	447	200
Kirbymoorside	1610	2828	2646	2278	1307	-53.4%	13,752	5052
Sinnington	924	1060	958	948	735	-30.6%	480	205
Totals:	**16,971**	**20,884**	**20,444**	**26,963**	**19,536**	**-6.5%**	**35,055**	**25,575**
* included with Gilling.								

Coxwold station from the road bridge east of the station, probably in the first decade of the 20th Century. As well as a train standing in the platform, another is approaching in the distance. (Author's Collection)

Gilling station before the new signal box was opened in 1906 when it was called 'Gilling Junction'. The goods train - probably the pickup - is hauled by NER Class 708 0-6-0 No. 730. (Peter J. Wheatley Collection)

Slingsby station between 1904 and 1914, with a passenger train entering the station behind NER Class A 2-4-2T No. 1598. (Author's Collection)

Kirbymoorside station between 1910 and 1914 with a train from Pickering, hauled by NER BTP 0-4-4T, possibly No. 988. (William Hayes)

A Pickering-bound train passing through Riseborough cutting, between Sinnington and Pickering, during the 1930s. The engine is a D20 4-4-0. (Raymond Hayes)

A train from Pickering entering Nawton station behind NER Class O 0-4-4T No. 2088 probably during the early 1920s. (Raymond Hayes)

A train calling at Husthwaite Gate station on the last day of the passenger service on 31 January 1953. The porter's face can be seen reflected in a window. (Neville Pick)

The quantity of goods traffic handled is an unsatisfactory measure of a line's or a station's economic health: much depends upon the despatch of specific types of traffic, often for short periods. The dramatic increase in Helmsley's tonnage in 1920 was due to the large quantity of timber that was extracted from the Duncombe Park estate during the years 1918-1920. The tenfold increase in Kirbymoorside's tonnage commenced in 1931 and lasted for several years. If Helmsley and Kirbymoorside are excluded from these calculations the picture looks less healthy, with an 11% fall between 1904 and 1927 and a fall of a similar amount between 1927 and 1934. It is evidence of a slow decline in the regular, run-of-the-mill goods traffic.

For the passenger business it was all gloom as the table below shows. In the early years there were around 325 passenger bookings from the Ryedale stations per day. If 'tickets collected' – *i.e.* journeys to these stations - are included there may have been about 600-700 passengers per day. The decline that had started before the First World War accelerated after its end, due to the expansion of bus services during the 1920s. The 'street' villages between Malton and Gilling - Hovingham, Slingsby, Barton and Amotherby – were especially vulnerable because the main road was more convenient than the stations. At these four stations as a whole there was a 61.4% decline in passengers between 1904 and 1927. Coxwold, Gilling, Helmsley, Nawton and Kirbymoorside were not immune and by 1934 they had lost a *further* 54% compared with 1927, or around 74% since 1904. It was an unhealthy situation, despite some stability during the 1930s.

The passenger earnings at the four stations between Malton and Gilling were £1,835 in 1923 and £538 in 1929. After estimating the value of the traffic that would be retained if the passenger service was withdrawn, a net annual saving of £486 was forecast. An internal memorandum concluded: 'the route between Malton and Hovingham is adequately served by an omnibus operator named Suddaby who is not associated with the Railway company... The

Nos. of passengers booked								
Station	1885	1904	1914	1920	1927	decline 1904-27	1934	1938
Husthwaite Gate	5060	5158	4454	4790	2328	-54.9%	1466	1598
Coxwold	7288	7329	6857	7748	4260	-41.9%	2006	2134
Ampleforth	3748	4124	3380	3577	1654	-59.9%	1515	1669
Gilling	8427	9043	7913	9303	5790	-36.0%	3720	4841
Hovingham Spa	10,150	9760	7298	7581	2958	-69.7%	+	+
Slingsby	7774	6622	6321	6478	3099	-53.2%	+	+
Barton-le-Street	3156	2903	2795	2954	1357	-53.2%	+	+
Amotherby	5024	5627	4642	4337	2203	-60.8%	+	+
Nunnington	6451	4485	3198	3768	2097	-53.2%	1258	1307
Helmsley	19,315	16,416	14,074	18,060	8791	-46.4%	3513	5379
Nawton	9149	9147	7865	10,357	5106	-44.1%	2470	2468
Kirbymoorside	20,679	20,191	17,710	21,436	11,426	-43.4%	5666	6274
Sinnington	9744	9109	8156	7606	2850	-68.7%	1740	1781
Totals:	**115,965**	**109,914**	**94,663**	**107,995**	**53,919**	**-50.9%**	**23,354**	**27,451**
+ excursion bookings only, included with Gilling.								

mail bag traffic is very light and the mails and newspapers can be worked to and from the Branch either by goods train service, where convenient, or by utilising the road service... Parcels traffic will for the most part be dealt with by the goods train service, but any urgent consignments will be sent forward by road service'. The final regular Gilling/Malton train ran on Wednesday 31 December 1930.

The end of this service received none of the attention that such an event would have received twenty years later. The *Yorkshire Gazette* reported on the arrival at Malton of the last train from Gilling at 7.15 pm, and that it 'comprised the engine and one coach and out of this there stepped only four passengers. The driver of the train was Mr Finan, who had driven trains on that branch for 20 years past... During recent years, however, the number of passengers on the line had decreased, and it was no uncommon occurrence for a train to arrive at Malton with two or three and sometimes no passengers at all'.

The total passenger numbers in 1929 for all thirteen Ryedale stations were 42,696, of which 5,165 (12%) were sacrificed by the closure of the four stations.

The line between Malton and Gilling was used by goods and occasional passenger trains, and the remainder of the Railways of Ryedale by both goods and passenger trains, for another 33 years. The Second World War brought much additional traffic, both passenger and goods, and this is described in Chapter 17. Following the end of the War there was a further inexorable growth in road transport and the decline continued. Unfortunately no figures of passenger or goods handled at individual stations are available for those years but the writing was on the wall for the passenger service.

Ampleforth station was closed to all traffic in June 1950 and in autumn 1952 rumours began to circulate that the passenger service between York and Pickering via Gilling was under threat. In November 1952 the *Yorkshire Illustrated* commented that 'local people realise that the number of passengers using the line are too few to make the running economical but they point to the fact that the transport facilities generally in the area are most inadequate'. The very geography of the line was its enemy. When a train from Pickering to York passed Sunbeck junction at Pilmoor it was geographically slightly further from York than it had been when it passed Gilling, ten miles earlier. The alternative Reliance bus service between York and Helmsley passed through the low-lying Howardian Hills; it was more direct and served other villages en route. A United bus service linked Helmsley and Kirbymoorside with Pickering.

Closure was announced for 2 February 1953, with the last day of service on Saturday 31 January, on the day when the notorious East Coast floods inundated considerable areas of eastern England. For the rail travellers the main memory is of people braving the gale force winds, lining the village platforms to bid farewell to the passenger train as it pulled out of their station for the last time. In the afternoon a chimney was blown off the Sinnington station house and through the glass verandah. That station was the only one to be closed completely that day.

Chris Wilson, a former pupil of Ampleforth College, made a special journey to York for the occasion. Initially he travelled from York to Pickering and then back again during the day, arriving back at York at 11.52:

I had brought some fireworks with me and I bought some flags at Woolworths with which to bedeck the train. At 5.30 p.m. I made my way over to Platform 12 for the 6 p.m. York-Pickering, the last passenger train to run on the branch. The Secretary of Leeds University Railway Society had fixed a wreath on the front of the engine, 'York, Gilling, Helmsley, Pickering 1853-1953', to which I added my flags. Passengers were photographed in front of the train. I began to distribute bangers to various people, though a member of LURS thought that this betrayed too much levity - yet they had brought a bottle of champagne to crack on the engine at Pickering. Apart from this frivolity there was little of note. D49 62730 Westmorland *was the locomotive. At Coxwold we passed the last Pickering to York train hauled by 62735* Berkshire.

Writing in *Trains Illustrated* in April 1953 David Bertram described how 'a green lamp shone, an engine whistled, and prompt to time, the 6.0 p.m. train to Pickering crept slowly out of Platform 12 at York. No state dignitary or idol of the cinema world was aboard to account for the unaccustomed buzz of activity surrounding its departure, however. Press photographers and amateur photographers were there, even the station master, resplendent in top hat, was on hand for the occasion... [At Pickering] prompt to time at 7.53 p.m. we came to a halt amid a crowd gathered on the windswept, gas-lit platforms... The station master formally declared the line closed, by breaking a bottle on the bufferbeam of No. 62730. The engine moved off into the darkness, the crowd dispersed and the railway enthusiasts and other sentimentalists repaired to the opposite platform to await the 7.50 p.m. train from Whitby'. The passenger service over the T&M between Gilling and Pilmoor had lasted for four months short of 100 years, and on the G&P for variously 82, 79 and 78 years.

With the end of the regular passenger trains, the six-and-a-half miles between Kirbymoorside and Pickering (Mill Lane junction) were closed completely and the track was reclaimed not long afterwards. The Raskelf Curve, the south curve onto the main line at Pilmoor (Bishophouse junction), was used by the occasional passenger train and the York pickup, until its closure in 1959. The remainder of the story of the Railways of Ryedale is recounted in Chapter 21.

The late J.W. Armstrong took the remaining photographs in this sequence, all on 31 January 1953. Here a morning Pickering train is waiting to set off from Gilling.
(J.W. Armstrong Trust)

The view from a Pickering-bound train as it enters Helmsley station. (J.W. Armstrong Trust)

LNER D49 4-4-0 No. 62735 Westmorland on the 7.25 a.m. York to Pickering at Kirbymoorside.
(J.W. Armstrong Trust)

D49 No. 62730 Berkshire *enters Sinnington, one of the very last trains to do so.*
(J.W. Armstrong Trust)

The 10.06 Pickering to York train, with D49 No. 62735 Westmorland, *crosses over to the down line at Pickering Mill Lane junction, prior to taking the Helmsley branch.*
(J.W. Armstrong Trust)

10 - Signalling

This description does not include the signal boxes at Bishophouse junction and Sessay Wood junction for the south and north curves at Pilmoor respectively, nor Mill Lane junction at Pickering. The word 'junction' is henceforward omitted from the names of the junction signal boxes.

Signalling on single lines has always been primarily concerned with preventing head-on collisions between trains running in opposite directions. When the T&M was first opened the stated aim was that only one train should ever be traversing the line at any one time, and that it should be accompanied by a nominated man wearing a red badge on his arm – a pilotman. This was relaxed to allow one train to follow another but only if the pilotman despatched the first and travelled on the second.

In 1862 the 'train staff' system was introduced on the T&M. It was introduced between Gilling and Helmsley in 1873 and from Helmsley to Pickering in 1875. Each line was divided into sections, for each of which there was a staff and each station was a staff station. The staff was given to the driver of a train. As long as the rules were obeyed and the driver *had the correct staff*, collisions were impossible. There was always a chance that the wrong staff would be given to a driver, which was dangerous, as well as inconvenient. This happened on 10 May 1881 at Kirbymoorside, as recorded in its occurrence book:

The 10.17 a.m. goods train from Helmsley arrived here at 10.55 a.m. carrying the wrong staff, he having the staff for the Gilling and Helmsley section, the proper staff having to be fetched on horseback, causing the 10.45 a.m. passenger train from Pickering a delay of 40 minutes.

A later sophistication of the staff system allowed successive trains to travel along the single line in the same direction; the driver of the first was given a ticket, of which there were several, *and shown the staff*. The driver of the last train was given the staff. This system depended on the signalmen at each end of a section knowing what trains were expected, so that they could organise the staff and tickets to ensure a free flow of trains. Roy Andrew was a clerk at Kirbymoorside when the section to Helmsley was still run with staff and ticket: 'when we had a relief signalman, the first thing he did in the morning was to reckon up the trains for the day. If there was anything special coming he had to take note because it would mean that he had to take a ticket out of the box and keep the staff'. Special, unscheduled trains were the problem. Occasionally a train arrived at one end of a section when the staff was at the other end, and there was no train coming in the opposite direction. The unscheduled train had to wait for another train to come through, or an engine had to be sent specially with the staff, if available.

The block system, using the electric telegraph, was introduced in 1881 and 1882. All stations were block posts, as were Sunbeck, Scarborough Road and Goslip Bridge (Pickering).

An example of a Tyers No. 6 Electric Tablet machine. (Author)

The inadequacies of the staff and ticket method caused it to be progressively replaced, in many cases by the Electric Tablet system. There was a machine at each end of a section, in which were placed a number of tablets, usually circular and from three to five inches in diameter. A tablet was withdrawn from the machine at one end of the section and carried by the driver to the other end of the section, where it was returned to the machine there. The tablet might also be returned to the machine from which it had been withdrawn, if the train went so far up the line and came back. This enabled another tablet to be taken out, either for another train in the same direction or for a train in the opposite direction. The tablet machines were interlocked so that a tablet could only be withdrawn from either machine when any previously-withdrawn tablet had been returned. As can be seen below, the tablets for each section had unique features to prevent them from being confused with, and used in error for, those of other sections.

Four fibre Electric Tablets and a metal Ticket. (Author)

Electric Key Token was an improvement on electric tablet working and was used between Helmsley and Kirbymoorside. Instead of a circular disc, the tokens looked similar to a key, and for each section were unique. The additional safety measure of having alternating sections of Electric Key Token and Electric Tablet prevented confusion on the part of the drivers. The points into some station yards were controlled from a ground frame which was unlocked by the tablet or key token.

The new systems were introduced at various dates; the stations named were block posts:

Electric Tablet:
1902 Sunbeck/Coxwold/Gilling
1904 Slingsby/Amotherby/Scarborough Road
1908 Kirbymoorside/Goslip Bridge (later Mill Lane)
1925 Gilling/Hovingham/Slingsby
1933 Gilling/Helmsley.

Electric Key Token
1933 Helmsley/Kirbymoorside.

An example of an Electric Key Token machine. (Author)

There was a mixture of signal boxes and platform frames. There were nine signal boxes, excluding those on neighbouring main lines at Pilmoor, Malton and Pickering. In most cases McKenzie and Holland lever frames were used; the electric tablet and key token instruments were Tyers.

Sunbeck. Opened in 1871 with 10 levers, later increased to 13 levers. A new lever frame with 25 levers was installed in 1904; reduced to 10 levers in 1932. Between the last train of stone to Thirsk on 3 February 1962 and the annual Ramblers' Excursion on 8 April 1962 no trains entered or left the T&M at Pilmoor. Sunbeck signal box still had to be opened so that a tablet could be withdrawn at Coxwold for the pickup, which went only as far as Husthwaite Gate. Come the summer, however, the regular flow of trains to and from the east coast commenced, preceded by nine days of drivers' route-learning specials, and there were also occasional passenger excursions. On most days the signalman seldom saw the trains that he signalled. The last summer Saturday train passed on 8 September 1962. Attendance was withdrawn from 8 October 1962 and the Coxwold to Sunbeck tablet was kept out of the Coxwold machine and became, in effect, a staff. Formally closed in 1964.

Coxwold. Probably opened in 1881 with 13 levers. The first signal box was at the west end of the down platform and it was described as a 'wood cover on platform' as at Hovingham, Slingsby and Amotherby (see below). Inasmuch as there were 13 levers – far more than those of those other stations – it may not have been the same design. A new signal box with 28 levers was erected on the then-new up platform in 1901. Closed in 1964.

Gilling. Probably opened in 1871 with 18 levers. It was at the west end of the down platform, adjacent to the level crossing. A new signal box with 52 levers was opened on the opposite side of the road in 1906. The levers were reduced to 30 in 1955 and it was closed in 1964.

Scarborough Road. Possibly opened in 1882, when block working was introduced between Gilling and Malton. The first signal box was immediately west of the bridge carrying the Scarborough road over the junction between the T&M and M&D. It had 12 levers. A new box with 34 levers was opened on Christmas Eve 1873; this was raised high above and east of the bridge so as to give a better view of the line on either side. Closed in 1964.

Helmsley. Probably opened in 1871 with 11 levers. It was a wood cabin at the south west end of the down platform. A new signal box with 25 levers was opened a few feet away, beyond the platform end in 1907. Closed in 1964.

Nawton. Probably opened in 1874 with 11 levers. It was a wood cabin at the east end of the platform. Closed as a block post in 1933.

Kirbymoorside. Probably opened in 1874 with 11 levers. It was a wood cabin probably on the down platform. A new signal box with 30 levers was opened close to the original in 1908. Closed in 1958.

Sinnington. Probably opened in 1875 with 11 levers. It was a wood cabin at the east end of the platform. Closed as a block post in 1908.

Goslip Bridge. Probably opened in 1875 with 9 levers and a crossing gate wheel. A new signal box with 16 levers and gate wheel was opened in 1906 close to the level crossing. It was closed in 1924, when the line to Mill Lane was singled and the latter became the block post for the section from Kirbymoorside.

With the introduction of tablet working three other stations remained block posts but had no signal boxes. The tablet instruments were in the station office and the levers were in a frame inside a cupboard-like wood cover on the platform. These stations were Hovingham (8 levers), Slingsby (8 levers) and Amotherby (7 levers).

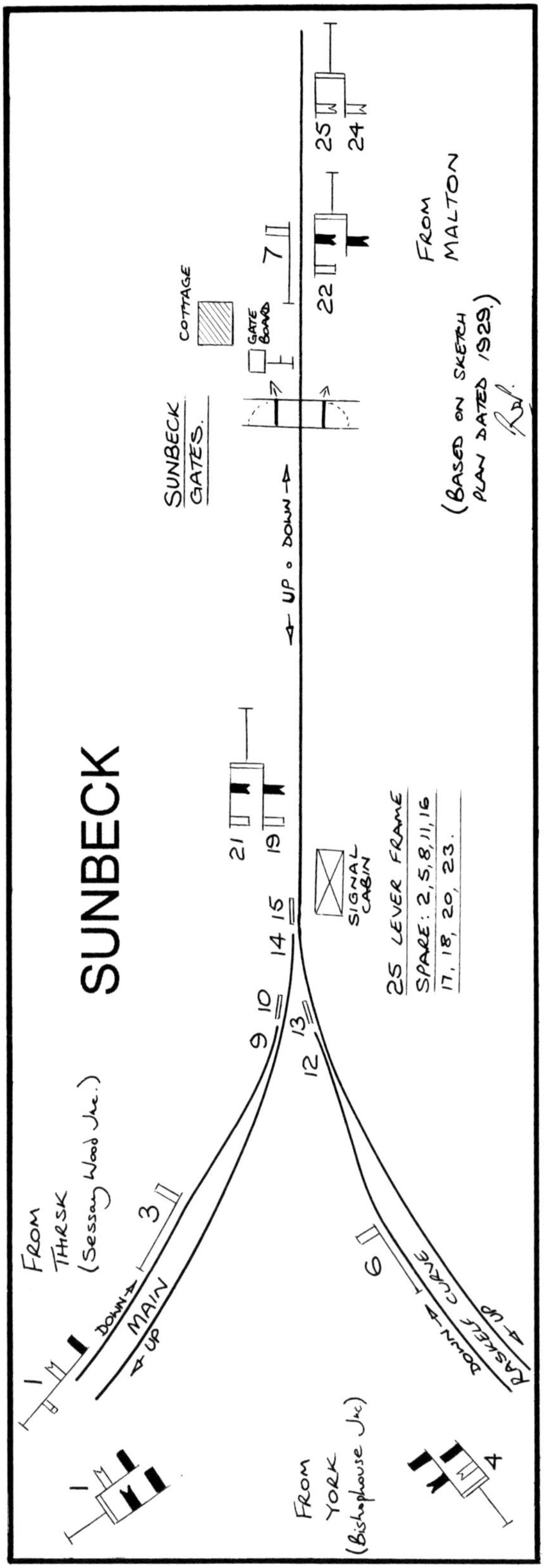

SUNBECK

From Thirsk (Sessay Wood Jc.)

← Down Main →
← Up →

From York (Bishophouse Jc.)
← Down Curve →
← Raised Up →

SIGNAL CABIN

SUNBECK GATES.

← UP • DOWN →

COTTAGE
GATE BOARD

From MALTON

25 LEVER FRAME
SPARE: 2, 5, 8, 11, 16
17, 18, 20, 23.

(Based on sketch plan dated 1929.)

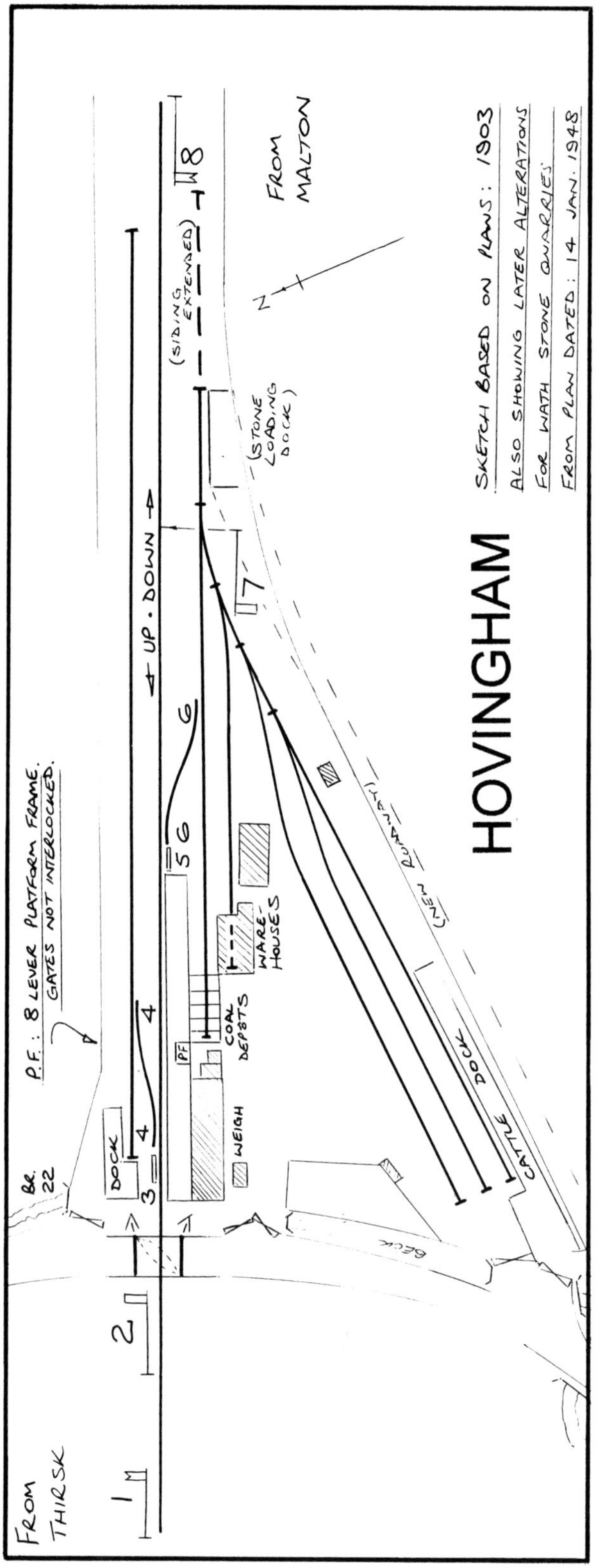

HOVINGHAM

From Thirsk

P.F.: 8 LEVER PLATFORM FRAME.
GATES NOT INTERLOCKED.

DOCK
WEIGH
COAL DEPOTS
WARE HOUSES

← UP • DOWN →

(SIDING EXTENDED)

STONE LOADING DOCK

CATTLE DOCK

(NEW PLATFORM)

BECK

From MALTON

N

SKETCH BASED ON PLANS: 1903
ALSO SHOWING LATER ALTERATIONS
FOR WATH STONE QUARRIES
FROM PLAN DATED: 14 JAN. 1948

Although Husthwaite Gate, Ampleforth, Barton-le-Street, Nunnington, Nawton and Sinnington ceased to be block posts they retained their block bells for a time, so as to be able to inform the next block post of a train's departure. These bell signals would also have been heard at any intermediate gatehouses (see Chapter 15). The signals remained at these stations and were operated from platform frames or, at Nawton and Sinnington, from the original small wooden signal boxes at the ends of the platforms. At Husthwaite Gate and Pye Pits the frames were on elevated platforms, although the former was once enclosed by the cupboard familiar elsewhere.

In changing tablets at any given point, apart from at Sunbeck, Scarborough Road and Mill Lane, a train would need to surrender one tablet and pick up another. Often it was a non-stop train and, as Tom Sharp relates from his time at Slingsby in the 1930s, the trains did not always slow sufficiently: 'it was the summer Saturday trains to Scarborough. Once they left Gilling they used to come sailing down. You stood at the edge of the platform to exchange the tablet. The fireman used to throw his tablet off and grab yours as he went past. They were supposed slow down to 25 m.p.h. which is fast enough, but some of them used to be going faster than that. The trains had big engines and I suppose that it went against the grain to travel so slowly along our little branch line. It was hair-raising. If they missed the tablet they had to stop.'

There were up to 30 tablets - notionally 15 per machine - for any one section so that, in theory, that number of trains could follow each other. When too many tablets accumulated at one end of a section they had to be transferred back by a lineman. This was a frequent occurrence when the summer trains to and from the coast were running on the T&M between Pilmoor and Malton. On the G&P it was rare and after 1953, when the line was taken up east of Kirbymoorside, there was normally never a shortage: a train going to Helmsley or Kirbymoorside had to come back again. But on one occasion a token transfer *did* take place, as Charles Allenby, clerk at Gilling from 1961 until six months before closure in 1964, explains:

For the last two years of the line's existence, every fourth Wednesday engineers would arrive at Gilling in order to begin the process of testing the points at Nunnington and Harome. Once the pickup had arrived back from Helmsley the Gilling porter signalman obtained a release from Helmsley which enabled a tablet to be withdrawn from the machine at Gilling. The engineers went by road with the tablet, firstly to Nunnington and then to Harome, to lubricate and test the points. When they arrived at Helmsley the tablet was returned to the machine there. Naturally, after a while the tablet machine at Gilling became nearly empty. On 4 July 1963 engineers arranged the transfer of fourteen tablets from Helmsley to Gilling. The engineers also tested the points at Nawton but the Annett's key they obtained at Helmsley was returned there afterwards.

The NER's policy was to have an inner junction, where a single line became double for a short distance before joining another double line. There was an inner junction at Sunbeck, for Bishophouse and Sessay Wood junctions, and another at Goslip Bridge for Mill Lane junction. These were worked on the absolute block system, in common with all double lines over which passenger trains operated. There was no inner junction on the T&M at its junction with the M&D at Scarborough Road; Scarborough Road itself was the M&D's inner junction with Malton East where it commenced.

In 1872, before the days of the telephone, the NER introduced a unique system for reporting faults in the bell system of communication. Gatehouses had 'repeaters' which enabled them to hear the block bell signals between the block posts on either side, but they could not transmit. An oval disc was placed in a prominent position on the outside wall of the gatehouse. It was reversible, with a black and a white side. If the bells were working properly the white side was left showing. The black side indicated a fault. The theory was that an engine crew would keep a look out and if they spotted a black disc they would report it at the next station. The system fell out of use in 1912 but invariably the discs remained in place, white side outwards, until the line closed more than 50 years later.

The primitive form of signalling at crossings on the T&M is exemplified by that at Broughton, with its Rotating Board Signal and the oval disc for reporting failures in the block system. (Author's Collection)

COXWOLD

SCARBOROUGH ROAD 1959

A diagram circa 1938 appears on page 26 of "The Malton & Driffield Junction Railway"

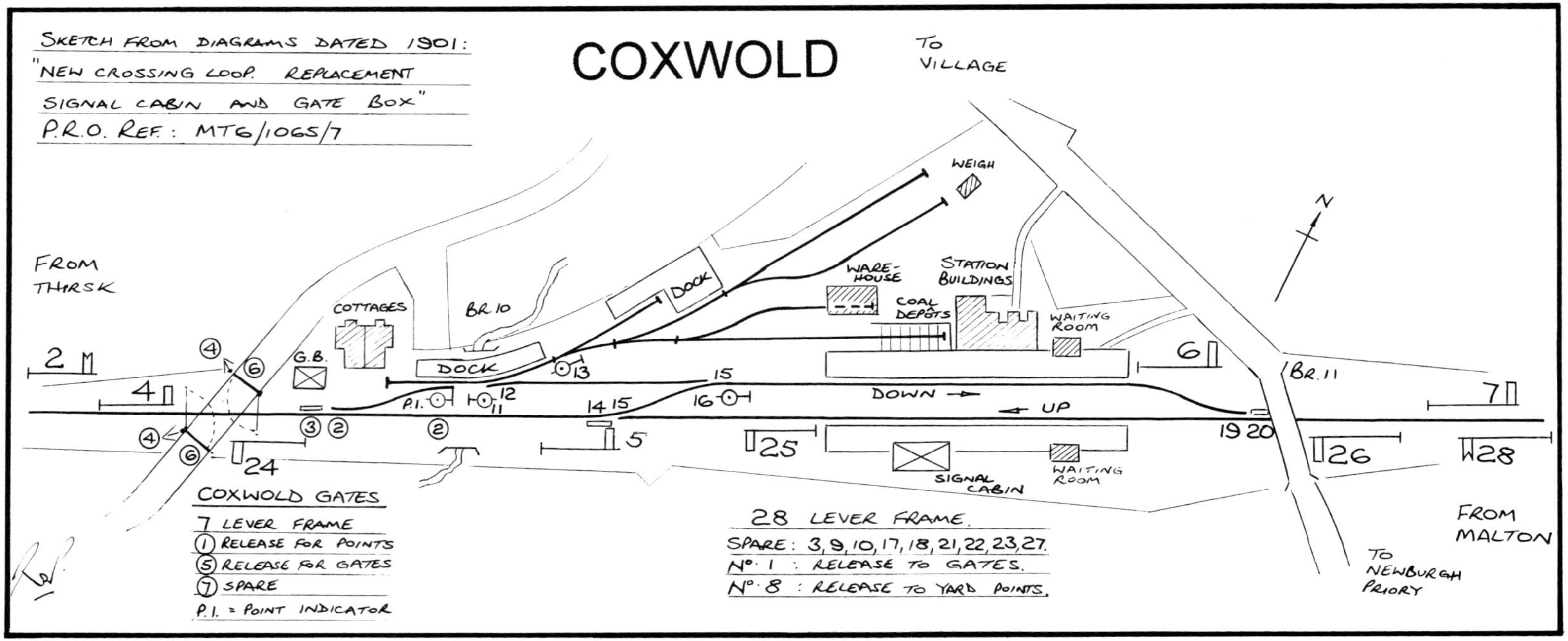

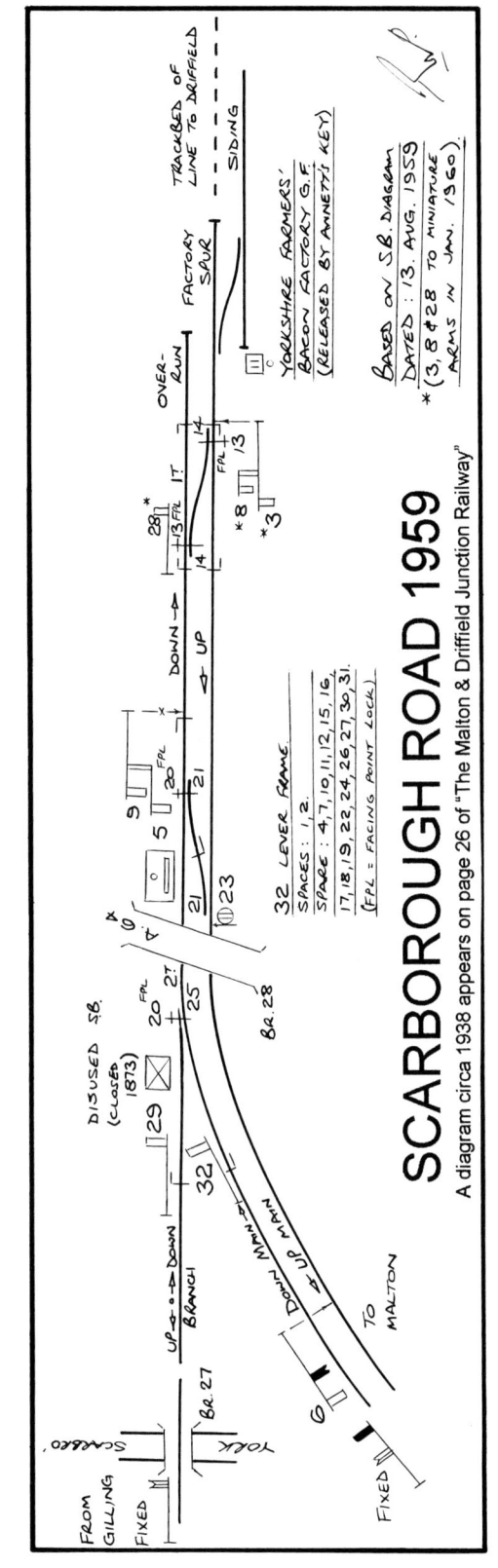

The decline following the end of passenger services in 1953 saw inevitable changes in signalling. After Kirbymoorside signal box was closed in 1958 the line from Helmsley became one engine in steam, with a train staff in the form of a key that unlocked the ground frames at Nawton and Kirbymoorside. Otherwise the electric tablet remained in use until the end.

The double line between Sunbeck and Sessay Wood was singled in 1960 and was controlled by a 'transient track circuit'. There was normally no current flowing along the rails and the relay was de-energised. When a train needed to travel over the line the relay was energised and the track was 'swept' by the sending signal box. If this process showed there to be an obstruction, the signals could not be released. If the line was clear the signals were released, allowing the train to pass. This remained in use until March 1963 and the severing of the junction.

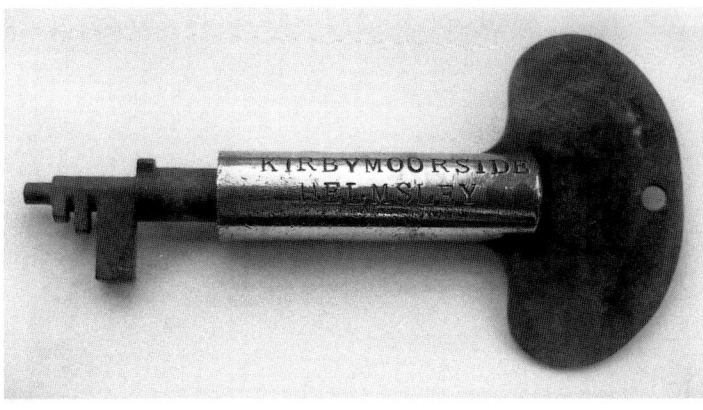

After the closure of the Kirbymoorside signal box in 1958 this Annett's key was used to unlock the intermediate siding at Nawton. (Author)

Early G&P Signal Boxes

Helmsley

Nawton

Sinnington

*Nunnington apart, G&P stations were equipped with small wooden platform signal boxes from their opening. Seen here are Helmsley, Nawton and Sinnington. Helmsley's was superseded in 1907 by the signal box portrayed under **Later Signal Boxes**, whereas those at Nawton and Sinnington remained until 1958 and 1953 respectively. Note the elaborate finials. (J.W. Armstrong Trust and Author's Collection)*

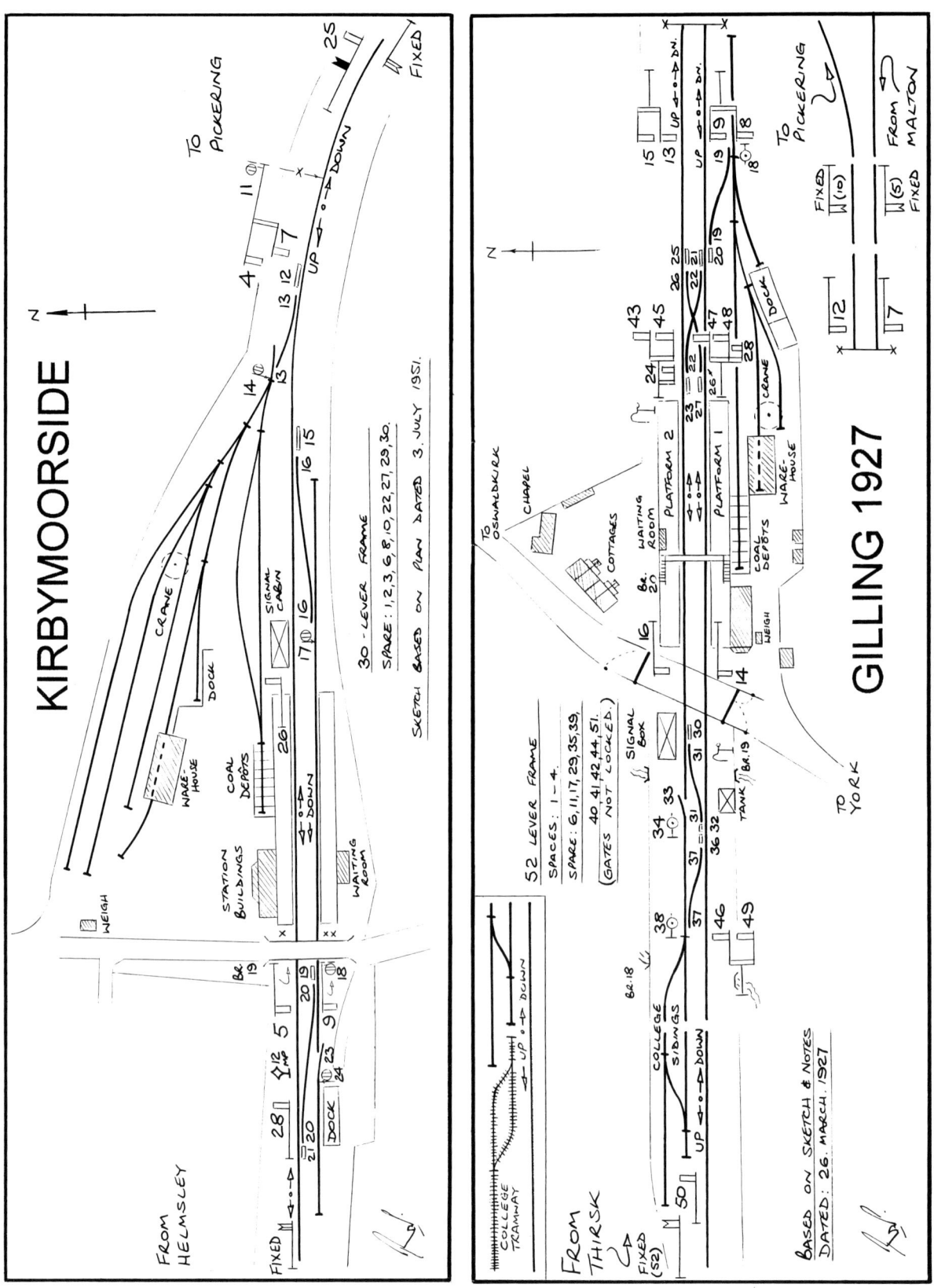

GILLING 1955
FIXED
50
DOWN SIDINGS
38
34
33
← UP. DOWN →
MAIN
TO YORK
46
49
37
31
30
AB 32
29
27
45
43
28
42
41
48
40
26
← UP. BRANCH. D^N →
← UP. MAIN. D^N →
FIXED
FROM HELMSLEY
FROM MALTON
25
24
GOODS YARD
GOODS YARD GF
N^O. 23 & (1) RELEASES
REVISED SIGNALLING
DIAGRAM DATED: 15. 4. 1955
GATES NOT LOCKED
30 LEVER FRAME (N^OS. 23-52)
SPARE: 35, 36, 39, 44, 47, 51, 52.

HELMSLEY 1951
FORMER TIMBER SIDING (PRIVATE)
GATE
STABLES
WEIGH
WARE-HOUSE
DOCK
COAL DEPOTS
S.B.
N
22
UP ← LOOP → DOWN
5
TO PICKERING
UP
DOWN
BR. 10
(1)
FIXED
W. ROOM
4
6
13
14
15
16
17
18
19
20
24
FROM YORK
UP
DN.
BR. 9
FIXED
(25)
7
10
9
2
8
SIGNAL BOX: 25 LEVER FRAME
SPARE: (1), 3, 11, 12, 21, 23, (25)
SKETCH AS AT JULY 1951.

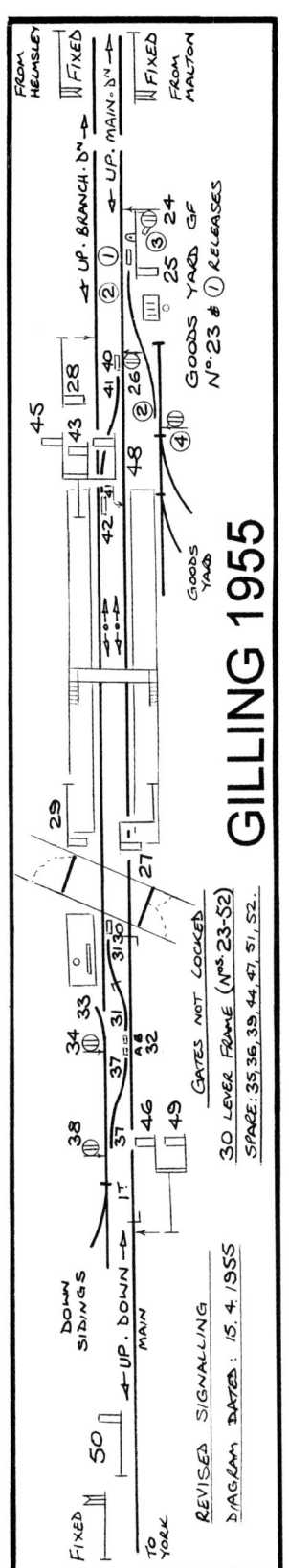

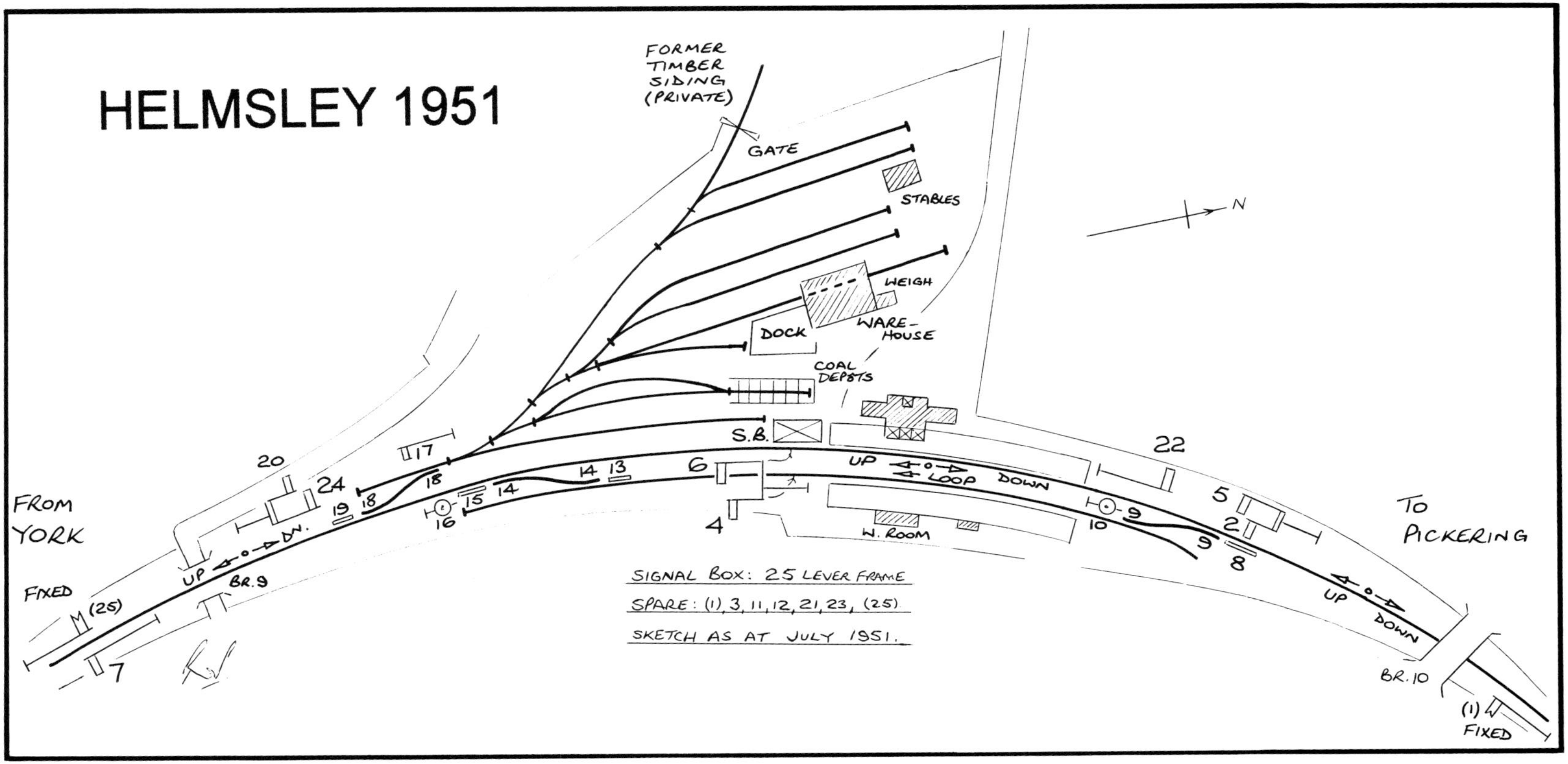

Early T&M Signal Boxes

Top Row: Sunbeck (left) and Gilling signal boxes, probably opened in the early 1870s, and with a distinct family likeness.

Middle row: The two signal boxes at Scarborough Road. Right: probably the oldest signal box on the Ryedale lines and originally glazed at the front. Its 1873 replacement, shown far right, was raised to three storeys to give the signalman a view over the adjacent bridge; it has gables and, unusually, glazed brick corners. It is clearly of the same pattern as Sunbeck and Gilling.

Several other stations had the cupboard-like platform frame. The interior shown left is of an example still in use at Hammerton on the York to Harrogate line. Several photographs elsewhere, including on pages 25, 29, 48 and 66, show the exteriors. (Author, Author's Collection and Frank Dean)

Later Signal Boxes

Four later signal boxes on the Ryedale lines all shared a family likeness, but with several slight differences. Upper: Coxwold (opened 1901), Gilling (1906). Lower: Helmsley (1907), Kirbymoorside (1908). Coxwold had no external walkway because, being on a platform, the windows could easily be reached for cleaning purposes. Kirbymoorside had a covered porch to the door. The configurations of steps vary, each being appropriate for its location. The steps to Helmsley signal box were renewed only a few years before closure. Unfortunately, they proved not to be long enough when received from the manufacturer; hence the two concrete steps at the bottom. Other photographs of these boxes appear elsewhere. No photographs of Goslip Bridge's two signal boxes have been located. (Author and Author's Collection)

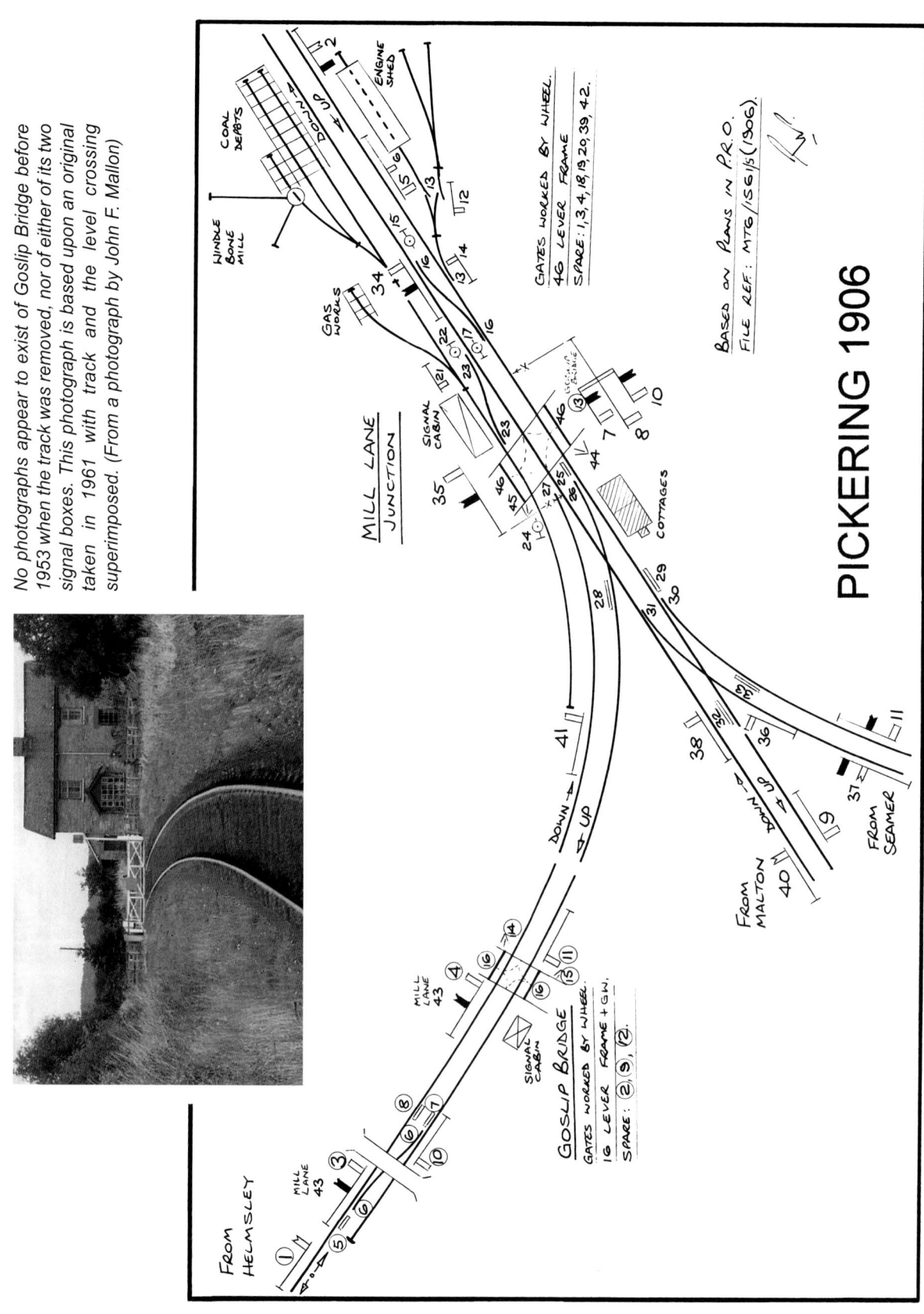

No photographs appear to exist of Goslip Bridge before 1953 when the track was removed, nor of either of its two signal boxes. This photograph is based upon an original taken in 1961 with track and the level crossing superimposed. (From a photograph by John F. Mallon)

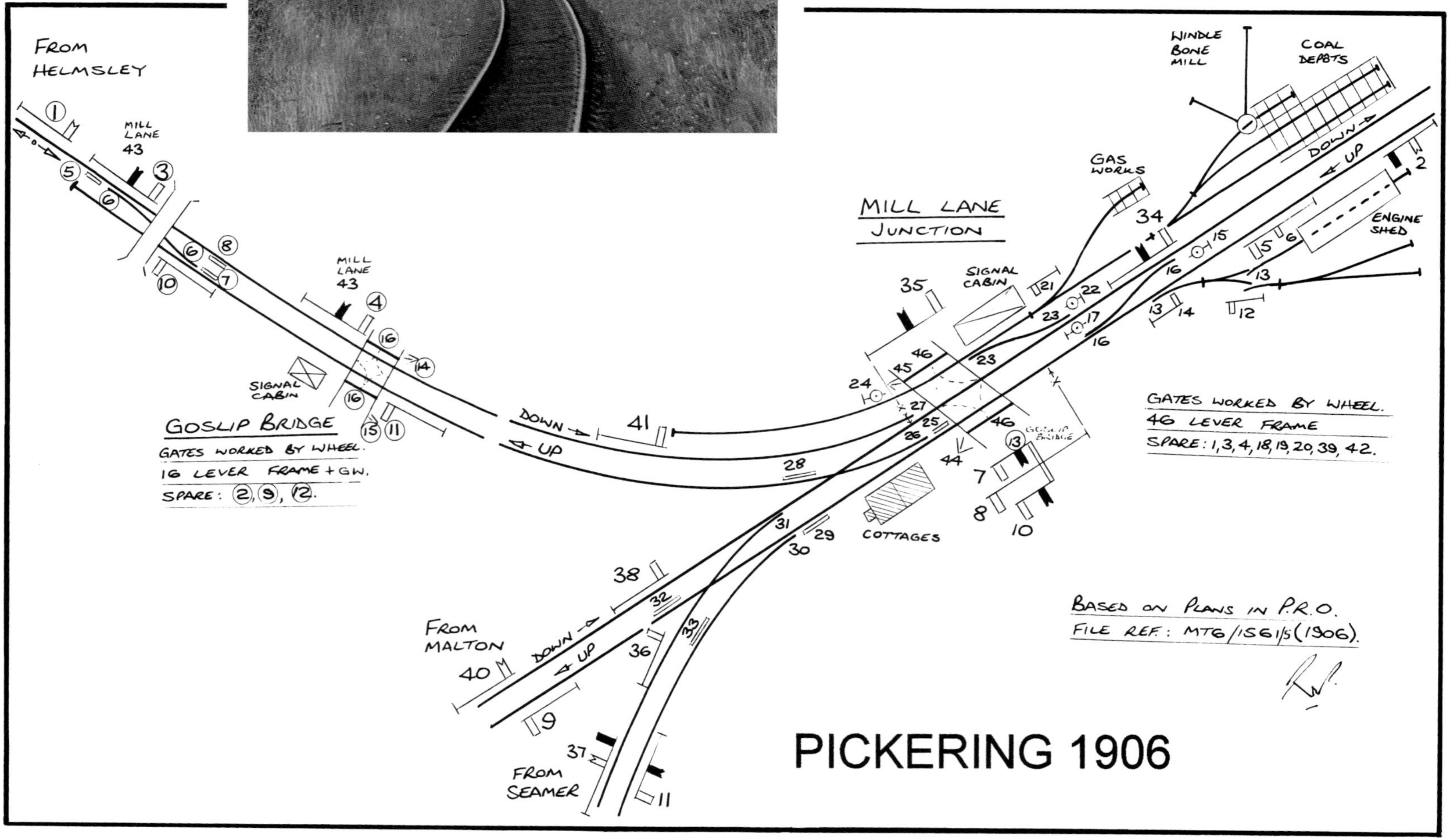

11 - Passenger Traffic

On the opening of the T&M in 1853 one passenger train shuttled between Thirsk and Malton, three times a day. The opening of the branch to Helmsley in 1871 saw an increase in the service, with four Malton/Thirsk trains with connections to and from Helmsley, and two Helmsley/Pilmoor trains. This pattern continued with the opening of the Helmsley to Kirbymoorside extension in 1874. There were no regular Sunday trains. The opening of the G&P through to Pickering in 1875 saw a service that began to exploit the potential of the new system, and contained a mix of trains between Malton and Thirsk, and between Pickering or Kirbymoorside and Gilling or York.

It will be recalled that under the 1865 agreement between the NER and the LNYD, the former undertook to provide 'quick trains' between Helmsley and York. This never happened on that route but they were tried between Malton and Thirsk at that time. It seems that the experiment was not a success: following a fatal accident at Ampleforth in December 1865 involving a non-stop 'Scotch Express' the Board of Trade report commented that such trains frequently ran without passengers. They were soon withdrawn.

By 1895 a complex pattern of interconnecting trains was based on the hub of the line at Gilling: Malton/Gilling and /Thirsk, and Pickering/Thirsk and /York trains. This service continued with changes until 1914 when it began to be reduced. By this time none of the trains went through to Thirsk but terminated at Pilmoor station. The basis of the service was two Malton/Pilmoor trains with connections from Pickering, and three Pickering/York trains with connections from Malton.

During the 1920s passenger carryings declined seriously and the service was further reduced. By 1923 the Malton/Gilling trains provided connections at Gilling into three Pickering/York trains and one Pickering/Pilmoor train. As the 1920s drew to an end the LNER introduced steam rail cars between Malton and Gilling. Ticket sales at the four stations between Malton and Gilling declined further and this service was withdrawn on 1 January 1931. In 1933 the service was that of 1923, but without the Malton/Gilling trains.

The Second World War saw an initial reduction to three Pickering/York trains, with morning and afternoon school trains between Helmsley and Pickering. As the War demanded more resources elsewhere, the service was reduced to one Pickering/Alne and one Pickering/Pilmoor train, with main line connections at Alne and Pilmoor; the mid-afternoon Pickering/Helmsley school train continued on school days but was not in the public timetable.

After the War, York once again became the destination for the trains. In 1950 there were three Pickering/York trains and the afternoon Pickering to Helmsley school train. In the last years the service was reduced further, with one of the Pickering/York trains running on Saturdays only. The school train continued to the end.

Ramblers' Excursions

Ramblers' Excursions were a popular late-spring and summer feature during the 1950s and 1960s. They took visitors along lines that mostly had no regular passenger service, such as to Ashbourne, Ingleton, Sedbergh, Hawes, Coniston and Kirbymoorside.

The Ramblers' Excursions to Kirbymoorside generally started at Keighley or Bradford. Until 1962 they ran up the main line from York, via Sunbeck and Coxwold, making the first stop at the last-named. For the last two years, 1963 and 1964, they ran via Malton, but this enabled people to alight there and at Hovingham. In these last years they ran under the evocative name of 'Special Ramblers' Daffodil and Primrose Diesel Excursion'. They used diesel multiple-units, which gave greatly improved views over the surrounding countryside. Most of the organised walks involved alighting at one station and rejoining the train at another.

In 1961 501 people travelled on the train. Thereafter the popularity declined, perhaps due to increasing car ownership but also perhaps the three-hour journey in each direction, which could be made by car in a little over half the time. The last Ramblers' Excursion ran on 3 May 1964 and carried 281 passengers, half of whom travelled to or from Kirbymoorside. This was the last passenger train to serve Nawton and Kirbymoorside stations.

Desmond Lee's excursions

In the mid 1950s Desmond Lee, the porter signalman at Helmsley, started to charter trains to take residents of the area on day excursions. Prior to that he had organised taxis to take local people to dances on Friday and Saturday nights as well as, for example, evening trips to Scarborough for the wrestling. Joe Hatfield, the station master at Helmsley, takes up the story:

Des Lee was full of enthusiasm. Initially when he ran his first one in 1954 or 1955 I helped him with the tickets, which were specially printed. Ken Claridge used to take Des all over the country on his motor bike, picking up five shillings a week from people at Gillamoor, Farndale and Bransdale, and all around the area. It was a farming community outing. Some of the farmers were quite affluent and they would take their wives and families on the annual outing. On the day of the excursion, Des went with the train of course. I looked after the station and worked the signals for the train – his train – then for the pickup later.

The excursions often used to come back at one or two o'clock in the morning. Hundreds of people would be milling about on the platform and in the yard, coming off the train or meeting families. It was quite a sight, although the lighting was rather inadequate on the platform.

The final Ramblers' excursion to Kirbymoorside, at Hovingham on 3 May 1964. The porter signalman, Eric Hartley, with the electric tablet in its pouch over his shoulder, is chatting to Charles Allenby, a local resident and previously clerk at Gilling station. (Author)

Right: A busy Nawton station for the last time on 3 May 1964 with the ramblers about to set off. A small group of local children are standing on the station's platform barrow on the right. (Author)

Below right: The scene at Kirbymoorside as its last passenger train stood in the platform on 3 May 1964. (John Spencer Gilks)

Page 66 upper:
Class B1 4-6-0 61216 passing Slingsby in 1961 with a Summer Saturday excursion for the east coast. The tablets are being exchanged by Fred Wright, the station's long-serving porter signalman. (David Sutcliffe)

Page 66 lower:
Class D49 4-4-0 269 The Cleveland, arriving at Kirbymoorside in August 1937 with a train from Pickering to York. (The signal was cropped off in the original.) (Colour-Rail)

One of the first destinations was Stirling and the Trossachs; in 1958 and 1961 to Largs, in 1959 Llandudno, in 1960 Great Malvern, in 1962 London King's Cross, in 1963 King's Lynn. The 1961 train to Largs started out from Kirbymoorside at 4.40 a.m. and arrived back fractionally under 23 hours later, at 3.33 a.m. the next day.

By this time there were no trains on the G&P during the hours of darkness and, therefore, none of the signal or station lamps needed to be lit. Desmond Lee's trains often did travel after dark and it was therefore necessary to light them. Helmsley station and signal box had gas lamps. Charles Allenby recalls that on 7 June 1963 'when the train came back from King's Lynn shortly before 1 a.m., the relief signalman had difficulty in getting the gas lamps lit. For a few minutes it looked as if he would have to contact the Gilling porter signalman, Gilbert Hugill, and advise him that the station might be in darkness when the train, and its load of several hundred passengers, arrived back. In the nick of time, however, he succeeded and the station was bathed in the warm glow of those three gas lamps that he managed to light. There was a wonderful atmosphere at the station that night, with the hissing of the gas lamps and the sense of anticipation before the train arrived'.

The train went on to Nawton and Kirbymoorside with the rest of the returning passengers. Desmond Lee himself lived in the station house at Nawton with his father, and alighted from the train – his charter – at Nawton when it returned empty from Kirbymoorside to York.

Norman Windress, the porter at Kirbymoorside, found the charters a mixed blessing: 'Once, after I came back from uncoupling the buckeye [between the engine and the first coach] on one of Des's trains at 4 am, my hair was so greasy that I had to wash it before I could go to bed. But it was good because for that train I got two special calls, at eight hours' pay for each call. It must have been very expensive to run those trains because we had our two special calls but also the crossings had to be manned'. These extra costs were incurred when other excursions ran.

On the closure of the Ryedale lines in 1964 Desmond Lee went on to found the successful travel agency, Ryedale Travel.

Scarborough excursions
There were annual excursions to Scarborough, often organised by the local Sunday Schools. The trains travelled empty from York, picking up at Coxwold and at all stations to Pickering or Malton and on to Scarborough. Apropos of the earlier years Ernest Watson recalled that:

When the Sunday Schools had their excursions to Scarborough the farmers used to decorate their horses and wagons and take their children to Nawton station. They took a pride in dressing the horses up with the horse brasses and different coloured ribbons. The Sunday School people used to give the children two shillings to spend, which was a lot of money. Then in the evening the farmers came down to the station to pick the children up again.

As a child John Smithson (later a clerk at Gilling) lived near Slingsby during the late 1920s and 30s and the annual Sunday School trip to Scarborough was an occasion to be relished: 'it was very popular because this was the only trip out in the year for many people. Part of each train was reserved for each village down the line. We had time on the beach, around the amusements and different things, lunch in the church hall in Aberdeen Walk, and you came back at night carrying all the presents that you'd bought. Relations and friends had given you money throughout the year for this trip so you set off with a pocket full of money, and you bought a lot of interesting things'. Appropriately, the last passenger trains ever to use the T&M and G&P were Sunday School excursions on Monday 27 July 1964.

Summer Saturday trains to the coast
Traditionally there has been much summer holiday traffic from southern Scotland and north east England to Scarborough. In 1932 it was decided to route these trains along the T&M, in order to avoid York. Entering the T&M at Pilmoor, they ran non-stop to Scarborough Road, pausing at Gilling only to take water. The awkward part of this operation was the need to reverse twice, at Scarborough Road and in Malton station. The Malton 'pilot' (shunting locomotive) pulled each train between the two, with the train engine remaining at the opposite end. The train then proceeded on its way to Scarborough. Coming from the coast the process was reversed.

In the years before the Second World War there were two such trains in each direction. On rare occasions they ran via Helmsley, Pickering, and Thornton Dale. In 1947, the year when the service was resumed after the War, Butlin's Filey Holiday Camp was opened, with its own station. For three summers the trains to Butlin's ran via the T&M and the M&D to Driffield, then up the coast through Bridlington, conveniently avoiding the three reversals which would otherwise have been necessary at Malton and at Seamer. Problems sometimes arose when a train was stopped at Wharram for the locomotive to take water, and it was found difficult to restart it on the M&D's 1 in 72 gradient. As the 1960s commenced the Summer Saturday trains were still numerous during the three months from mid-June to mid-September. There were 74 in 1959, 73 in 1960, 66 in 1961, 59 in 1962. The last train of the 1962 season, from Scarborough to Newcastle on 8 September, was the last train to use the main line junction at Sessay Wood.

In the peak summer holiday period of 1937 there was also a daily train between Middlesbrough and Scarborough via the T&M. This circuitous route was chosen so as to relieve the more direct Coast route via Whitby. The train departed Middlesbrough at 9.10 a.m. and arrived at Scarborough at 12.01 p.m. It left Scarborough again at 7.25 p.m., taking two hours, thirteen minutes for its return journey, about half an hour less than the route via Saltburn and Whitby. In summer 1938 there were three such daily trains from Redcar via Middlesbrough to Scarborough. After the War this service was resumed and continued until 1954. Its operation was spasmodic, however, and it seems to have only run when required by the numbers of people wishing to go from Middlesbrough to Scarborough.

Other special trains

Many other excursion trains travelled the line and this account cannot be exhaustive. In 1902 and 1906 – and probably in other years too - the NER ran special trains to and from Hovingham for the two-day Hovingham Musical Festival. For the 13th Festival, on Friday 8 August 1906 a train left Malton at 1.53 pm for Hovingham. After the evening performance two special trains took the visitors home: one to Malton, where there were connections for Scarborough, York and Leeds, and another to Pickering via Gilling. On showing their festival tickets to the booking clerk they were able to buy return tickets at one fare and a quarter from stations within a radius of 60 miles of Hovingham.

In May 1963 a three-car diesel multiple-unit brought a party from Fylingdales Early Warning Station from Scarborough to Helmsley (and on to Whitby). It was the last passenger train to call at Nunnington.

Finally, there were occasional trains of railway enthusiasts. There were two during June 1957. The Branch Line Society's *Yorkshireman* was the first, on 2 June. It started at York and went up the main line to Alne, where it traversed the Easingwold Railway. It joined the T&M and ran to Kirbymoorside, back to Gilling and continued to Malton. It went by the M&D over the Wolds to Driffield, Market Weighton, Selby, Church Fenton and back to York. The second train was for the Railway Correspondence and Travel Society on 23 June. Starting from Leeds it went to York and joined the T&M at Sessay Wood. Like the earlier train it went to Kirbymoorside, back to Gilling

The last local excursion to Scarborough picking up its passengers at Helmsley on Monday, 27 July 1964. (Author)

The scene at Gilling as the last two Sunday School trains to Scarborough - on the right from Helmsley, on the left from Gilling - on 27 July 1964. (Author)

and on to Malton and the M&D. From Driffield it went north to Filey and Scarborough, then to Whitby and back to Leeds.

The last was for the Stephenson Locomotive Society on 1 October 1963, as part of a multi-day railtour of the north-east. From Whitby this train ran down the coast to Scarborough, then to Malton. It traversed the remaining parts of the T&M and G&P: Malton - Gilling – Kirbymoorside - Gilling – Coxwold - Gilling - Malton. It went on to Grosmont, Middlesbrough, Hawes and York via Ripon later the same day.

Page 71 upper: The gatehouse and cottage at Pockley Gates, whose country quiet in latter days was disturbed only by the once-daily pickup to Kirbymoorside and very occasional excursion. (David Sutcliffe.)

Page 71 lower: Class V2 2-6-2 60839 standing at Gilling station on 1 May 1962, on a train of Ampleforth College students which has just arrived from London. (Tom Worsley)

Slingsby - the last passenger train, 27 July 1964. (Author)

A Summer Saturday train passes through Slingsby behind English Electric Type 4 No. D254 on 28 July 1962. (Ken Hoole)

LNER

ATTRACTIONS IN YORK:
Theatre Royal—SIR FRANK BENSON AND COMPANY.
MARTINMAS PLEASURE FAIR.

ATTRACTION IN LEEDS:
Rugby League Football Match—HUNSLET v. YORK.

EXCURSION TO YORK & LEEDS

On Saturday, 24th November, 1923,

From the undermentioned stations at the times stated:—

			Fares there and back Third Class.	
			To York.	To Leeds.
		a.m.		
Pickering	... dep.	11 25	4/8	7/5
Sinnington	...	11 35	4/8	7/5
Kirbymoorside	...	11 45	4/4	7/-
Nawton	...	11 50	4/-	6/8
Helmsley	...	11 58	4/-	6/5
		p.m.		
Numington	...	12 5	3/7	5/11
Gilling	...	12 15	3/2	5/7
Ampleforth	...	12 24	2/10	5/3
Coxwold	...	12 30	2/7	4/11
Husthwaite Gate	...	12 35	2/5	4/9
Raskelf	...	12 45	1/8	4/9
Alne	...	12 50	1/5	4/8
Tollerton	...	12 55	1/3	4/5
Beningbrough	...	1 5	1/-	3/11
York	...	1 20	—	3/2

The train will return the same day at the following times:—

| Leeds (New Station) | ... | ... | dep. | 9 35 p.m. |
| York | " | " | " | 10 30 " |

TICKETS CAN BE OBTAINED IN ADVANCE.

NO LUGGAGE allowed. CHILDREN over 3 and under 12 years, half-fares.

TICKETS are not transferable; are only available to and from stations for which issued and by excursion trains in both directions; are not available for intermediate stations; must be obtained before travelling or full ordinary fare will be charged; are issued subject to General conditions and regulations specified in the Company's current time tables.

Tickets can be obtained at the Stations, also at York from Messrs. THOS. COOK & SON, 38 Coney Street.

For further information apply to the District Passenger Manager, York (Tel. No. 264).

116—Yorkshire Herald Co., York—2,500.

BRITISH RAILWAYS

RAMBLES IN THE NORTH YORK MOORS NATIONAL PARK

by the RAMBLERS' ASSOCIATION

Special Ramblers' Daffodil and Primrose Diesel Excursion

TO **COXWOLD HELMSLEY NAWTON and KIRKBY MOORSIDE**

SUNDAY 8th APRIL 1962

Light refreshments will be available in each direction.

Rail Fares—Second Class

OUTWARD			Coxwold	Helmsley	Nawton	Kirkby Moorside
		a.m.	s d	s d	s d	s d
Bradford (F. Sq.)	...dep.	9 50	11/-	13/6	14/-	14/6
Skipton	"	8A 50	14/3	16/3	17/3	17/3
Kildwick & C.	"	8A 58	13/6	15/6	16/6	16/6
Keighley	"	9A 6	12/6	15/-	15/6	15/6
Bingley	"	9A 11	12/-	14/-	14/6	14/6
Shipley	"	9 55	11/-	13/-	14/-	14/6
Newlay	"	10 5	10/6	12/6	13/-	13/6
Kirkstall	"	10 10	10/-	12/-	13/-	13/6
Huddersfield	"	8B 42	12/6	14/6	14/6	15/6
Mirfield	"	8B 51	12/-	13/6	14/6	15/-
Dewsbury (Well. Rd.)	"	8B 58	11/-	13/-	14/-	14/-
Batley	"	9B 1	11/-	13/-	13/6	14/-
Leeds (City)	"	10 25	9/6	11/6	12/6	12/6
Cross Gates	"	10 35	8/6	11/-	12/-	11/-
Garforth	"	10 40	8/-	10/6	11/-	11/-
Selby	"	9C 48	7/-	9/6	10/-	10/-
York	"	11 10	4/6	6/6	7/6	8/-
Coxwold	arr	11 55	Passengers Return same Day only as shown			
		p m				
Helmsley	"	12 25				
Nawton	"	12 35				
Kirkby Moorside	"	12 40				

RETURN

		p m
Kirkby Moorside	...dep.	7 0
Nawton	"	7 5
Helmsley	"	7 15
Coxwold	"	7 50
York	...arr.	8 34
Selby	"	10C 22
Garforth	"	9 6
Cross Gates	"	9 12
Leeds (City)	"	9 20
Batley	"	10B 24
Dewsbury (Well. Rd.)	"	10B 29
Mirfield	"	10B 35
Huddersfield	"	10B 43
Kirkstall	"	9 32
Newlay	"	9 36
Shipley	"	9 45
Bingley	"	10A 4
Keighley	"	10A 9
Kildwick & C.	"	10A 19
Skipton	"	10A 27
Bradford (F.Sq.)	"	9 52

NOTES:— A—Change at Shipley   B—Change at Leeds (City)   C—Change at York

FOR DETAILS OF CONDUCTED RAMBLES, PLEASE SEE OVER

Published by British Railways (North Eastern Region) 2/62 Printed in Gt. Britain Jowett & Sowry Ltd. Leeds 1   BB5

R 3149(HD)

*A Glasgow to Scarborough Summer Saturday train entering the T&M at Sessay Wood junction, whose signal box can be seen behind the rear, on 13 August 1960. The right-hand track by this time was disused. The engine is B16 4-6-0 No. 61435.
(John F. Mallon)*

*A 10-coach Scarborough to Glasgow train approaching Coxwold, with V2 2-6-2 No. 60879, on 21 July 1962.
(Bernard Scotson)*

*English Electric Type 4 (later Class 40) diesel locomotive No. D389 passing through Gilling on 30 June 1962 with a train from Glasgow to Scarborough.
(Tom Thackray)*

Page 75 upper: An array of tickets. Those in the top two rows were found in the drawer in Kirbymoorside - see Chapter 7. (Author)

Page 75 lower: A model of Sinnington station made by Mike Cook. The equivalent of an aerial photograph, this faithfully shows the layout of the station building, similar to that at Kirbymoorside. The G5 0-4-4T engine regularly worked the push-and-pull on this route. (Barry Norman in Railway Modeller)

Left: The Branch Line Society's visit to the Ryedale lines on 2 June 1957 was hauled by D20 4-4-0 No. 62387. It is seen here at Gilling.
(J.W. Armstrong Trust)

Right and below: The RCTS visit in 1957, three weeks after that of the BLS, was in the charge of D49 4-4-0 No. 62731 *Selkirkshire*, and is seen at Kirbymoorside (right) and at Gilling (below). The former shows the porter signalman, Harry Young, handing the electric key token for the single line section from Helmsley to the crew. (Harry Young and Author's Collection)

004
COXWOLD TO 2
Kirbymoorside
First Class
For conditions of issue see back. N.E.R.
Kirbymoorside TO 1
COXWOLD
First Class
For conditions of issue see back. N.E.R.
004
030
PILMOOR JUN. TO 2
Kirbymoorside
Second Class
For conditions of issue see back. N.E.R.
Kirbymoorside TO 1
PILMOOR JUN.
Second Class
For conditions of issue see back. N.E.R.
030
003
AMPLEFORTH TO 2
Kirbymoorside
Third Class
For conditions of issue see back. N.E.R.
Kirbymoorside TO 1
AMPLEFORTH
Third Class
For conditions of issue see back. N.E.R.
003
097
Soldier on Furlough
Foreign To
KIRBYMOORSIDE
Via
THIRD CLASS
See back. N.E.R.
SOLDIER on Furlough
KIRBYMOORSIDE
Foreign To
S.onF.
Via
THIRD CLASS
See back. N.E.R.
097
003
16DAYS EXCURSION
Return as per bills.
EDINBURGH, N.B.
To
KIRBYMOORSIDE
VIA BERWICK.
THIRD CLASS
See back. N.E.R.
16 Days EXCURSION.
16DysEx EdinburghNB
Kirbymoorside
To
EDINBURGH, N.B.
VIA BERWICK.
THIRD CLASS
SEE BACK. N.E.R.
003
KIRBYMOORSIDE
Kirbymoorside TO Kirbymoorside
HARTLEPOOL WEST STATION.
Hartlepool W. Hartlepool W.
016
First Class N.E.R.
Issued subject to regulations in time tables.
KIRBYMOORSIDE
Kirbymoorside TO Kirbymoorside
HARTLEPOOL WEST STATION.
Hartlepool W. Hartlepool W.
000
Second Class N.E.R.
Issued subject to regulations in time tables.
2nd-PRIVATE DAY EXCURSION
27th July, 1964 (S.T. H913)
Helmsley Joint Sunday Schools
CHILD
Scarborough to HELMSLEY
(N) For conditions see over
PRIVATE DAY EXCURSION-2nd
27th July, 1964 (S.T. H913)
Helmsley Joint Sunday Schools
CHILD
Helmsley to SCARBOROUGH
(N) For conditions see over
0033
2nd-SINGLE SINGLE-2nd
0024
CHILD
York to
York Gilling for Ampleforth
York Gilling for Ampleforth
GILLING for AMPLEFORTH
(N) 3/0 Fare 3/0 (N)
For conditions see over For conditions see over
CHILD
0024
1148
BRITISH RLYS. (N) For conditions see back
Available for three days including day of issue
BRITISH RLYS. (N) For conditions see back
Available for three days including day of issue
Nawton Nawton
NAWTON to YORK
YORK YORK
Via MALTON or RASKELF
3rd. 7s.1d.Z 3rd. 7s.1d Z
1148

SINNINGTON

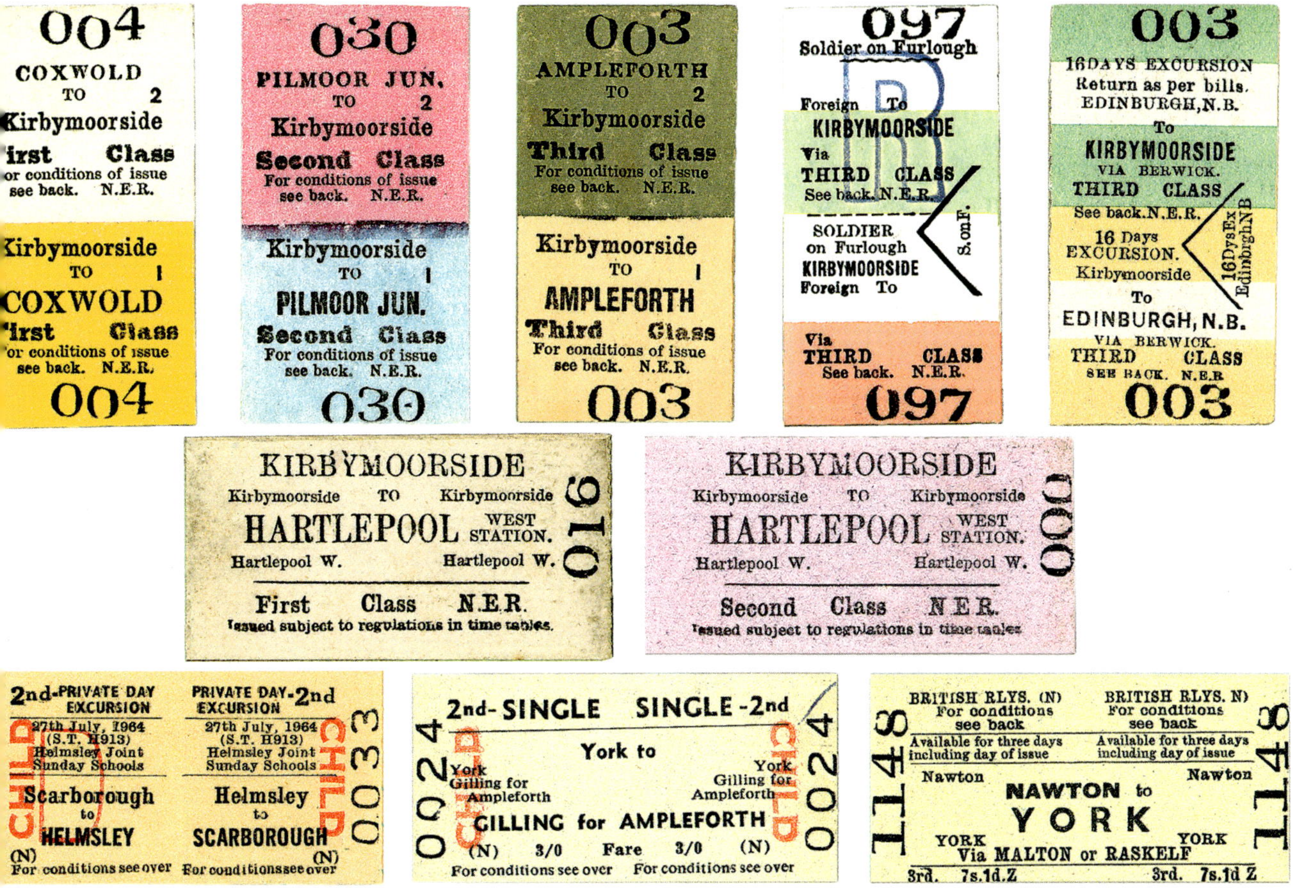

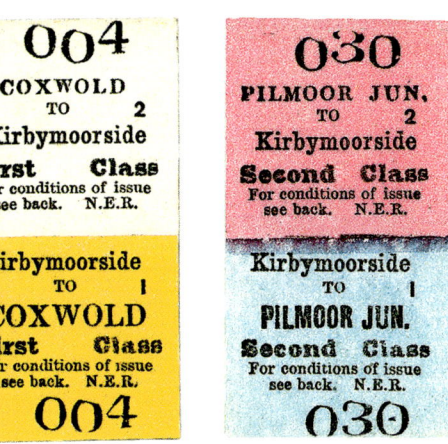

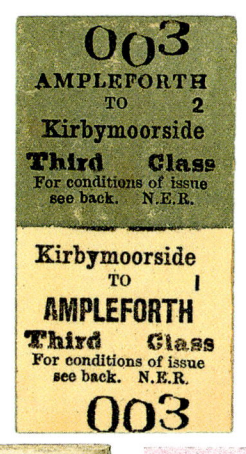

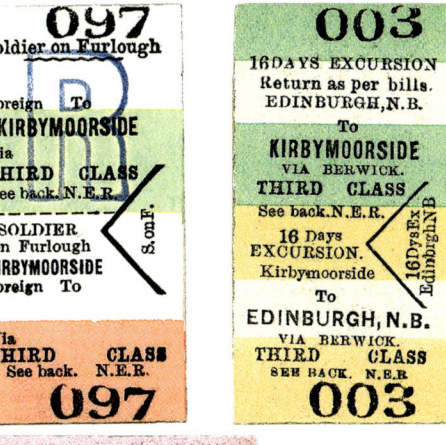

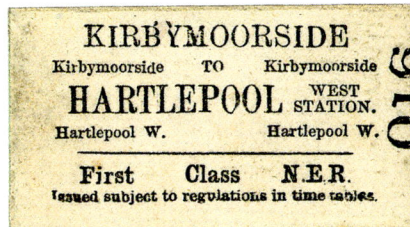

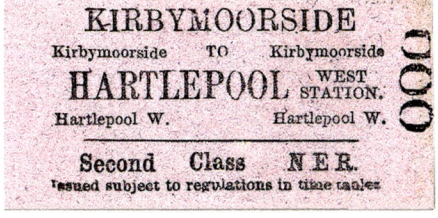

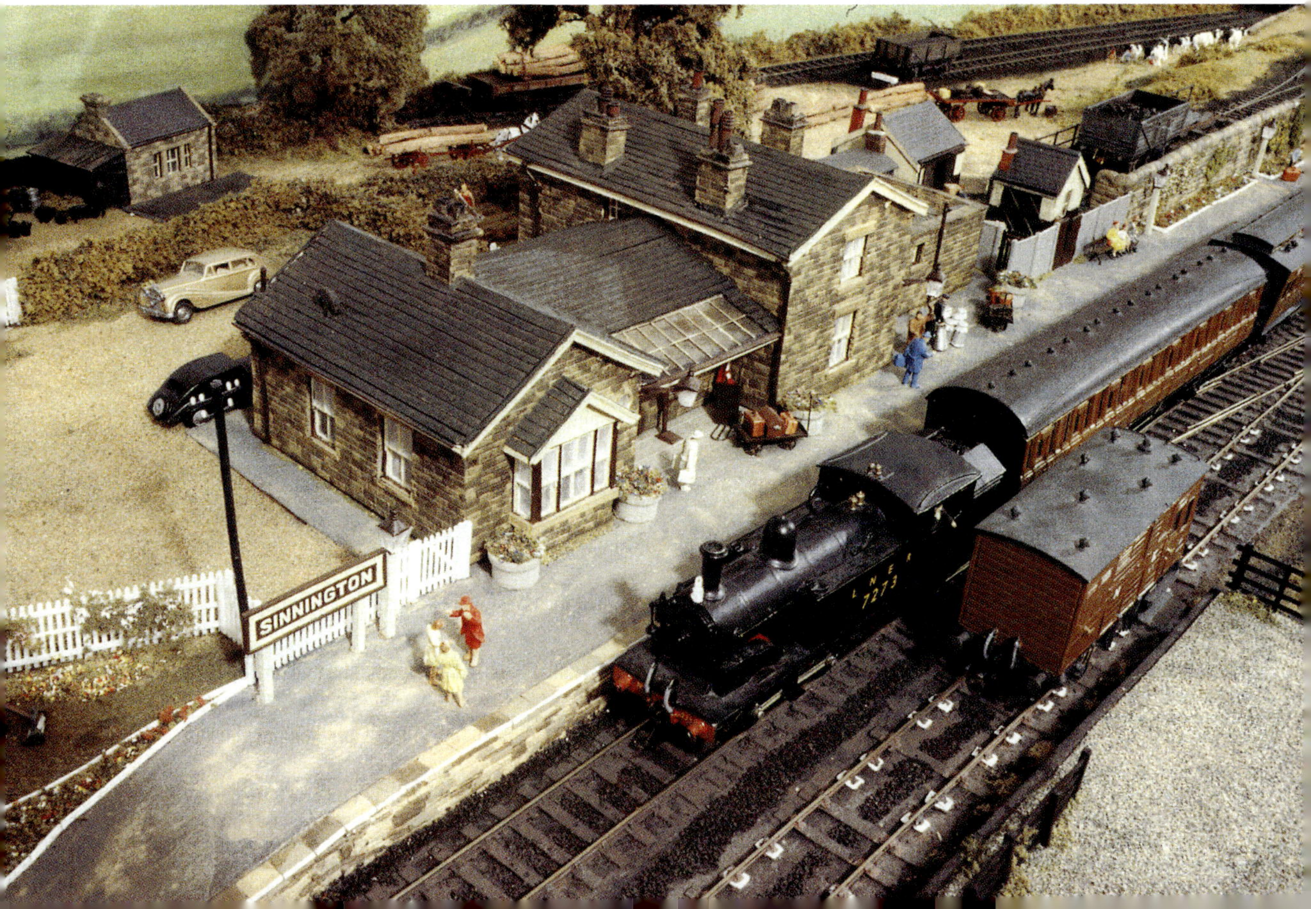

12 - Ampleforth College

Ampleforth Abbey and College stand on the southern escarpment of the Hambleton Hills. Gilling Castle, the College preparatory school, is at Gilling East. From the early years Gilling station was the College railhead, having better facilities than Ampleforth station. To the boys of the College the trains were symbolic: they bore them reluctantly from their parents at the start of each term and they returned them joyfully to the family bosom at the end. Chris Wilson, a former pupil, provides a romantic recollection:

On still mornings the valley was filled with mist and one could frequently hear the guard's whistle blow at Gilling station, doors being shut and then all those clanks and wheezings which were the hallmarks of branch line locomotive workings. Where patches of mist had lifted, one might get a glimpse of the tubby coaches and squat locomotive. At night the gaily-lit carriages threaded their way through the various woods. Occasionally the open firebox door and the flaming plume of steam could be seen.

Until the early 1930s the College pupils used the local passenger services but, as numbers grew, the LNER was persuaded to run special trains to and from Gilling. For the railway authorities the College specials created their own agonies, as Frank Hick recalls: 'We had to be really on our toes as some of the hierarchy at Ampleforth were friendly with the General Manager, Mr Jenkin Jones. It was always quite a major effort to get the luggage and the boys in an orderly way into the trains. It was a very important job and we had to work it very efficiently, otherwise all hell was let loose. If anything went wrong, they went straight to the General Manager'. In the early days Father Lambert was responsible for the arrangements. Later, and until closure in 1964, it was Father George Forbes.

Through the 1950s and 1960s two trains were run at the beginning and end of each term: from and to King's Cross and either Leeds or Liverpool. At the end of the summer term the destination of one train varied, according to where the Cadet Corps summer camp was taking place: Brancepeth, County Durham in 1961; Shorncliffe, Kent in 1962.

The College provided regular work for the staff at Gilling station, including Audrey Hugill, a clerk there during the Second World War:

The Ampleforth College chauffeur, Jimmy Winder, used to come down with people for the first train in the morning, and meet them off the last train at night. There was nearly always someone from the College for the first train. Also a man came down from the College with a van every day, to take the parcels. Summersgills of Helmsley were leading coal all day long to the College. One day a woman came off the train from York at half past eight, for an interview as a cook at the College. She had brought her 18 cats with her, in crates. She hadn't paid for these, so I had to calculate the excess fares. No-one had come down from the College to meet her so we rang them up to tell them. Jimmy Winder came down to collect her and the 18 cats, and he was down again for the next train; she hadn't got the job!

By the early 1960s, the regular passenger service had been withdrawn and, for the staff of Gilling station, the six-times-a-year College specials provided a highlight in a goods-orientated existence. Charles Allenby was the only clerk at Gilling during the last two and a half years. The trains consisted of a loco-hauled train to King's Cross and a diesel multiple-unit to Leeds:

At the end of the College terms there was a tremendous amount of work, booking tickets and luggage. Each term the College account came to about £1,300, for tickets and luggage. For the luggage we - the porter signalman, Gilbert Hugill, and I - went to Gilling Castle first and then the College. Gilling Castle was usually a Saturday morning's job, and we booked the luggage in two or three hours. We would go up to the College after work, two to three days before the end of term. We stuck the parcels stamps on the trunks and marked each one with a number – 1 to 5 – according to which luggage van it was to be loaded into. A few days before the end of each term six luggage vans were brought in by the pickup and put into the yard, where they were loaded by Summersgill's. Five of the loaded vans were removed by a special parcels train.

At the end of term the loco-hauled train arrived empty from York on platform 2 - the north platform. The engine ran round and attached the accompanied luggage van, which had been loaded in the yard and placed in the College Siding the day before by the pickup. It then drew forward again into platform 2 and College students then boarded.

About 40 minutes later the empty DMU from York or Leeds arrived at platform 1. About 20 minutes after the DMU arrived, the King's Cross train set off for Malton and York. Another 20 minutes after this the DMU, now loaded with departing students, set off.

At the beginning of term, the DMU from Leeds came first, at about 6.30 p.m. into platform 1. About 30 minutes later the train from King's Cross arrived at platform 2. It pulled far enough forward to clear the crossover east of the station. This enabled the DMU, once the tablets had been exchanged, to return to York, empty. The luggage vans arrived on the pickup.

The last College trains, from King's Cross and from Leeds to Gilling, ran on Tuesday 28 April 1964, three-and-a-half months before the final closure of the line.

In 1870 the Prior of Ampleforth asked the NER to provide a station and a siding at Ampleforth College Gate, on the T&M immediately below the College. The NER agreed to the station but only provided that the College built a platelayer's cottage and laid an access road. Neither station nor cottage was ever built but in 1895 the NER agreed to a three-foot gauge tramway being laid from Gilling station to the College.

Ampleforth College Specials

Father George Forbes OSB in his role as the Ampleforth College cadet force chaplain, overseeing the departure of the special train conveying the College's cadet force to Brancepeth, County Durham, on 28 July 1961. Father George had earlier served in the Grenadier Guards. The engine is V2 No. 60938. (Bernard Scotston)

A London-bound College special loading at Gilling in December 1958. The engine is about to run round to the other end of its train prior to leaving for Sunbeck, Pilmoor and the main line. (Bernard Scotston)

On another occasion, 22 July 1960, V2 No. 60856 has picked up the boys' accompanied luggage van and run round. The homeward-bound boys are about to join their train. (Bernard Scotston)

The College had started to produce its own gas, consuming about 500 tons of coal per annum. About 200 tons of goods were also sent to the College annually and, during one of the regular periods of expansion, building materials too.

The company extended the College Siding so that goods could be transhipped direct from wagon to wagon. From the College Siding the tramway was laid along the edge of the T&M for 1,000 yards, using the swathe of land that had been purchased, but never used, for a second track. It then turned to the north, up the hill to the College, becoming steep as it approached the gasworks. A short branch led to a brickworks.

Two horses working in tandem were the usual form of haulage; one was sufficient for most of the two miles from Gilling station but the final haul up to the gasworks demanded two. Building contractors used internal combustion locomotives and in the final years the College acquired its own similar locomotive.

As none of the wagons had brakes, runaway wagons were not unusual, as reported in *The Ampleforth Journal* in 1909:

Three times this term has the gate near the old cricket ground been completely shattered by runaway trucks. On one occasion only has the whole school witnessed this thrilling sight - for such it really was. A large iron truck heavily laden was seen bearing down at full speed upon the closed gate. The momentary excitement turned to entire surprise when it passed through the five bars and crossbars as though it had encountered no obstacle. It was as well for the horses approaching from Gilling with more trucks, that it soon left the lines and rolled over into Mr Perry's hayfield. The spectacle was quite entertaining and well worth a gate...

Passengers were carried for some years. There was a special passenger wagon, described as 'more like an open charabanc with railway wheels'. About 20 boys would go in this vehicle. Goods wagons were also used: sacks were laid inside to prevent the coal dust getting on the boys' clothes. In 1915 *The Ampleforth Journal* published a short extract from a poem, with added editorial comment:

Now I wonder if I dare
To say this railway needs repair,
Or to suggest it's in decay!
For what would then the owners say?
But if the government would only
Nationalise this railway lonely,
Oh! Far better would these trucks be
Which convey both you and me.

We hasten to add that the general sentiment is one that would be enthusiastically re-echoed and endorsed by the members of the 12th Reserve Cavalry Regiment, who on their return journey by 'this lonely railway' found themselves precipitated in the dark into the hinterland of the 'rugger' field. We offer them our apologies and sympathy.

In 1923, the College switched to electric lighting and later the gasworks was closed. The agreement with the LNER was terminated in April 1929 but the tramway had fallen out of use some years before.

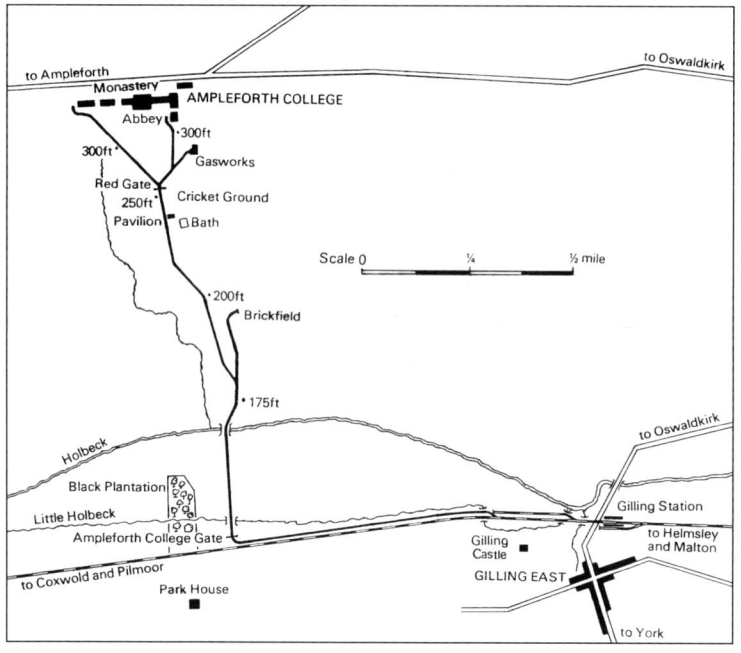

The Ampleforth College Tramway. (Map drawn by Mike Swift)

The Ampleforth College Tramway

The tramway was seldom photographed, as it was closed by the mid-1920s. As far as is known the photograph above is the only one of it in action, though it appears posed. Two tubs of coal are seen where there was no gradient, most likely up at the Abbey as the NER line cannot be seen. (Ampleforth Trustees)

Temporary extensions to the tramway were made when earth had to be moved about to create more playing fields. As a source of cheap (and enthusiastic?) labour, schoolboys may be unrivalled. A group of about a dozen are seen left and below setting to with a will to excavate for a new playing field, probably in about 1907.
(Ampleforth Trustees)

371.　　　　King's Cross to Gilling—Special.
　　　　　　Malton to Scarboro' Road—Light Engine.
　　　　　　Gilling to York—Empty.

	A	G			C
	p.m.	p.m.			p.m.
King's Cross	1 26	—	Gilling..		7†25
Doncaster	4 37	—	Coxwold		7 40
Shaftholme	4 44	—	Sunbeck		7 55
Selby	5 0	—	Pilmoor		7 57
York	5 18	—	Thirsk		8 12
,,	5 25	—	,,		8 32
Malton	5L53	—			SL
,,	6 1	5∥57	Skelton		9 13
Scarboro' Rd.	6 5	6∥0	York (Clifton Sdgs.)		9†18
,,	6 9	—			
Amotherby	6 17	—			
Slingsby	6 23	—			
Hovingham	6 27	—			
Gilling..	6 38	—			

　　　Stock—BSO, 3 TSO, Cafcar, 3 TSO, BSO, BG (Detached at Gilling).
　　　Conveys Ampleforth College Students.

The internal BR Special Traffic Notice for the Ampleforth College train from King's Cross to Gilling on Monday, 20 September 1960, at the start of the autumn term. The train travelled via Malton and during its 47 minute stop at Gilling it shunted the vehicle carrying the boys' luggage into the College siding. It returned to York via Sunbeck and Thirsk, where it reversed.

13 - The School Run

Many of the local children went to grammar schools by train: those from Ampleforth, Coxwold and Husthwaite to Easingwold; those from Gilling to Amotherby inclusive, as well as Nunnington, to Malton; those from Helmsley to Sinnington inclusive to Pickering.

The pupils who went to Easingwold Grammar School travelled to Alne where they changed into 'The Coffee Pot' - the train for Easingwold. Millie Watson of Ampleforth was one: 'In the morning I left Ampleforth at a quarter past eight and arrived at Easingwold at a quarter past nine. School didn't start until half past on account of the children travelling by train. We left school at half past four and the train departed Easingwold station at about five o'clock to Alne, and then on the main line to Pilmoor, where we changed again back to Ampleforth arriving at about half past six'.

John Harrison was one of about a dozen who went from Hovingham to Malton during the 1920s: 'the school train was the normal service train, which stopped at Hovingham at about half past eight, picking us up. It was a long way up from the station to the Malton Grammar School'. Those pupils who travelled to Malton could only use the train until the passenger service ended on 1 January 1931. Bill Young, the brother of Doris Otterburn, went from Nunnington to Malton Grammar School between the ages of 11 and 17, also during the 1920s:
He left home in Nunnington every morning at half past seven and didn't get home until seven at night.

The train left Nunnington at about eight o'clock and he had to change at Gilling and go on to Malton. It was over a mile from Nunnington to the station and there were three seats; they used to call them 'first seat', 'second seat', 'third seat'. You had a good view right across Ryedale. If he got to 'third seat' and could see the little train leave Nawton he knew he just had time to get to the station before the train. He got into school at nine.

They used to do awful tricks in those days. Once my brother was coming home from school and, as usual, changed at Gilling. When the other boys got off at Nunnington, they'd left him fastened on the luggage rack, tied up. They found him at Helmsley and got him off. I don't know how he got home from Helmsley.

Many more pupils travelled to Pickering. They used the normal train services between York and Pickering, morning and afternoon. On the outbreak of war in 1939 an unadvertised schoolchildren-only Helmsley to Pickering train took them in the morning, arriving in Pickering at 9.10 a.m.; another unadvertised Pickering to Helmsley train took the children home, leaving Pickering at 3.50 p.m. and reaching Helmsley at 4.15. Although these trains were intended for the schoolchildren, others could and did use it. The morning public train from York was resumed in the late 1940s and lasted until the end of the passenger service in 1953 but the afternoon schoolchildren-only train remained. Betty Watson remembered from the late 1930s '20 getting on at Helmsley, 10 or 15 at Nawton, quite a lot more at Kirbymoorside'. Eric Wrightson travelled to school from Kirbymoorside: 'we used to arrive at school a little bit later and we therefore got a shortened lunch break. The girls travelled in so many compartments and we boys travelled in the others. This was compulsory, as directed by the school. Coming back the station staff at Pickering warned that, if there should be any mixing, they would hound them out'. Reg Sleightholme, a pupil during the early 1930s, was one of 'no more than six of us on the school train from Sinnington. It was quite a long walk from Pickering station to Lady Lumley's and we used to make that last as long as we could, so that we might possibly miss morning assembly, if the train was a few minutes late!' Judy Barker (née Sturdy) went from Kirbymoorside to Pickering from 1946, when she was 11, until 1951:

Three of us from Kirby started in my year. There were also two in the next form and about three or four in the fifth form, say about 15 in all from there. 99% of the passengers were school children. It was known as the School Train but we used to get occasional intrepid travellers on it who were not going to school.

On the first day I got a lecture from my Mum, to stay on the platform, not to go near the end of the platform, not to go anywhere near the engine. By the time I got on the train I was about petrified! We lived at the top end of Kirbymoorside and I had to walk down to the station. If it was a wet morning you got soaked on the way down. We had to wear regulation school gaberdines, pork pie hat, nylon stockings and black shoes. You sat and steamed on the train and then got soaked again. It was a wonder we didn't get pneumonia.

We used to resent it when the snows prevented the kids who came by bus from getting to school. The trains got through, so we got through too. In winter 1947 though we couldn't get through and we were off school for weeks.

It was always very cliquish on the train: certain people sat in certain carriages; boys never sat with girls, ever, until they got to about the upper sixth. The boys sat in separate compartments, with their books in a small suitcase, and they used to play cards all the way to Pickering and all the way back.

The pupils of the later years tended to recall the fun – or the mischief – that took place on the school trains. Judy Barker was one of these:

The tricks we used to play were very juvenile! If there were any messages we wanted to pass to one another we used to open the window and lean right out and shout 'Oi!' We had to shout as loud as we could and, depending on whether the person in the next compartment heard or not, he or she used to come to the window. There were about five of us in a gang who went in a compartment together. We would dare one another to sit up in the luggage racks when we went through Sinnington station so that the people getting on there would think it was an empty compartment and get in. No-one ever did so we never found out.

Once I made a gooseberry fool at school and brought it home. It looked revolting and so a girl called Valerie, who had been brought up in India and was also a bit of a tearaway, decided to throw it out of the window of the train, at Richard Boddy. It missed him but, as the train was moving, it shot all down the length of the train. People thought it was sick!

Occasionally there would be a fight and one of our school caps or hats would go flying out of the window. We would then go home and ask Dad to drive us back to Sinnington, 'three fields on from that telegraph pole', to pick it up. Mum used to play war as they were quite expensive.

On one occasion pupils from Lady Lumley's went to the Eskdale Tournament of Song Music Festival at Whitby. Judy Barker and Richard Boddy were amongst them. Richard Boddy: 'we were throwing our caps about. I was standing in the middle of the compartment and someone was throwing my cap at me. Of course someone else at the wrong moment opened the window. I missed the cap and out it went somewhere in Newtondale'. Judy Barker: 'we all had to sing with our hats on and Richard had to stand on the front row with his great mop of black hair and no cap on. We all got into bother about that. He didn't get that hat back. At the competition we finished the song exactly together, all 40 of us in the choir, for the first time ever. We won the competition and a big banner'.

It is not surprising, perhaps, that the school train was known by the clerks at Pickering as 'the monkey train'. For all that these were childish pranks, accidents did happen. There was normally a melée as the children – boys mainly – jumped onto the running boards as the train drew in Pickering station and tried to find an empty compartment. Caroline Strickland fell down between two carriages and lost her arm.

The children forged a very good relationship with some of the train guards. One, known only as Joe, was remembered by Judy Barker: 'he was a nice old bloke, very friendly. The inspectors used to get on quite frequently and check our passes. If you were caught going on to Nawton when you should have got off at Kirby there was always a bit of bother but Joe would allow you to, and to sit in the guard's van as well. Occasionally they would all get in the guard's van and ride to Helmsley and back. I never did as there would have been a war if I didn't arrive home when I should.'

In the months leading up to the end of the passenger service in 1953 the North Riding County Council was about to open a new secondary school immediately next to Nawton station. The North Eastern Region of BR pointed out that, although one end of the schoolchildren's journeys might be well-sited for the railway, the other end often was not: children came from villages and farms, often several miles from a station. Overall, it was insufficient to keep the whole line open.

14 - Goods Traffic

The pickup was a long-standing feature of country railway operation. In a routine that remained unchanged for decades, each pickup started from a station that received and despatched fast goods services from other railway centres. It then proceeded from station to station dropping off and picking up wagons as it went along. In 1856 a daily goods train operated each way on the T&M, threaded between the three passenger trains and stopping at all stations. This was supplemented by a mineral train in 1860.

Completion of the G&P through to Pickering demanded a service to each station from all parts of the rail network. This was achieved by providing for the transfer of wagons from one train to another. In 1875 a goods train ran from Malton to Gilling, then to Helmsley and Pickering. A second train ran from Thirsk to Gilling, connecting with the first train at the latter. In 1895 there were three pickups, all to Gilling: from Scarborough via Pickering, from York via Malton, from Darlington via Coxwold. All three were in Gilling simultaneously between 12.25 and 12.50 and the process of sorting wagons out from one train to another can only be imagined. To make matters even more complex, between 11.25 and 11.35 there were four trains at Gilling station simultaneously: the Darlington pickup, two Pickering/York passenger trains and a Malton to Thirsk passenger train. A cattle train ran from Pickering to Gilling and back on alternate Tuesdays.

By 1914 the focal point had moved to Helmsley:

arrivals		via
11.18	Darlington goods	Coxwold, Gilling
12.10	Malton goods	Malton, Gilling
12.30	Scarborough goods	Pickering
departures		*via*
12.25	Darlington goods	Gilling, Coxwold
1.00	Malton goods	Gilling, Malton
2.00	Scarborough goods	Pickering

On their return from Helmsley the Darlington and Malton pickups followed each other to Gilling where they exchanged wagons between the two parts of the T&M. A Tuesdays-only cattle train ran from Malton direct to Pickering and back via Helmsley and Gilling. In 1938 wagons were transferred between the pickups at Gilling and Kirbymoorside. The end of the York/Pickering passenger service early in 1953 saw the closure of the Pickering to Kirbymoorside section of the G&P; the York pickup ran to Gilling and the Malton pickup to Gilling, Helmsley and Kirbymoorside. The York pickup was cancelled in May 1955 and Husthwaite Gate and Coxwold stations were served by the Hovingham stone trains (Ampleforth station had been closed to goods in 1950). Following the cessation of the stone trains in early 1962 a solitary pickup from Malton served all stations as required. Wagons for the Kirbymoorside branch were left at Gilling while the pickup went to Coxwold and Husthwaite Gate, and back. From April 1963 until the line closed in August 1964 this pickup ran on only three days a week (Monday, Wednesday and Friday).

The Pickup - Steam Hauled

The pickup calling at Gilling with J39 0-6-0 No. 64928 shunting on 26 May 1960. (John Spencer Gilks)

The pickup with J27 No. 65844 shunting in Helmsley goods yard on 18 October 1961. On the right is a former road wagon, now a fixture of the station yard and marked on the side 'NOT TO LEAVE HELMSLEY'. The configuration of the doors can be clearly seen. (Hugh Ballantyne)

Right: In the last years of the Ryedale lines there was time for the return pickup to stop at Nunnington station - by then a public delivery siding and the station building a café - for coffee and cakes. J39 No. 64928 is gently simmering alongside on 26 May 1960. (Alan Lillywhite)

Below: J27 No. 65844 is coming into Helmsley station with the pickup on 18 October 1961. On the platform, and turning to look at the train, is Desmond Lee, the porter signalman and organiser of annual excursions. (Hugh Ballantyne)

The Pickup - Diesel Hauled

On 5 August 1964 the pickup has arrived at Coxwold and the driver is throwing the single line tablet, in its pouch, to the porter signalman, Cyril Sherwood. (Author)

Later on the same occasion, all four wheels of a lowfit wagon on the pickup became derailed at the entrance to Coxwold yard. The wagon was re-railed by the crew and the station staff, including Cyril Sherwood seen walking purposefully around the rear of the derailed wagon. A schoolboy is watching avidly. (Author)

Small parcels and packages were carried in 'road wagons' attached to the pickups. According to Frank Pickett, the road wagons were 25-tonners with two sets of doors: a drop door at the bottom which formed a ramp and two swing doors at the top. When Roy Andrew was a clerk at Helmsley in 1918 'the road wagons all had their specified routes. One was Northallerton to York via Gilling and Helmsley. It would come in on the Thirsk goods, on to Pickering on the Pickering goods, and then on to York via Malton. There was one from Northallerton to Hull, which also came on the Thirsk goods, to Pickering, Malton and then on to Driffield. While the train was at your station you had to hunt for the goods inside the wagon. Usually it would be at the platform and a porter went into the wagon with a wheelbarrow and unloaded our packages. The invoices were supposed to be in a box on the wagon side but sometimes they had been lost so you always had to look through in the wagon and see what there was for you.'

Coal

The NER encouraged its station masters to run coal businesses on their own accounts. The company earned money from the carriage of the coal to stations, as well as demurrage – rental – for the station coal cells and from the wagons if they were retained longer than a minimum period. For the station master himself it was a lucrative sideline, especially so at Helmsley and Kirbymoorside. The station master at Helmsley from 1935 to 1943, Harold Naylor, was renowned for his enthusiasm for the coal sale. Roy Andrew was a clerk there during some of the War years:

During the War coal, like everything else, was in short supply. One morning I came into the goods office at Helmsley and Mr Naylor was doing a jig! I stopped dead and said 'what's wrong?' He was almost doing the sailor's hornpipe with joy: 'there's a wagon of South Kirkby coming; there's a wagon of Whitwood coming!' There were a lot more pressing items of railway work to be dealt with but, to him, coal was more important.

After Harold Naylor's departure from Helmsley in 1943 the coal sale was put into the hands of a depot agent, Ron ('Ponner') Hill, formerly a clerk at Kirbymoorside. This was also done at Kirbymoorside with Harry Lee, previously a clerk at Pickering, but in the last days the station master once again took over the business. At some stations the income exceeded that from the station masters' railway employment and tended to keep them there for extended periods. The Gilling station master also had the coal sales at Hovingham, Slingsby, Barton-le-Street and Amotherby, following the removal of their station masters in 1926. Tom Thackray, the last incumbent, was there from 1948 until closure in 1964.

The station porters helped with the labour of weighing and shifting coal, some well rewarded by the station masters, others not. Audrey Hugill: 'Mr Thackray was always generous to the staff who helped him with the coal business, for example in weighing coal out to his customers when he wasn't there. He paid people like Fred Wright at Slingsby £20 or £30 a year for looking after the coal'.

Animal feed

The warehousing and distribution of animal feeding stuffs was a staple item at many country stations. The products of each company were stored either in the general goods warehouse or in one set aside for the purpose. The keeping of the records, the ordering of stocks, the unloading of the wagons and the distribution to farmers: all were the task of the station staff. The feed was ordered, despatched by rail to the station and subsequently collected by the farmers or delivered by the railway delivery service. An agent for the feed company solicited orders from the farmers and visited each station periodically to check the stock.

Helmsley, in the centre of an agricultural area, handled much such traffic. The Brandsby Agricultural and Trading Association opened a warehouse specifically for feed in 1914. Later, they were joined by Bibby's, Crossfield and Calthrop, Lever's, B.O.C.M., Silcock's (and non-feed in the form of Earle's Cement). Norman Race describes the traffic and some the problems encountered with it:

There were nine or ten wagons a week for Bibby's, about a wagon a week for Silcock's, and Lever's to a lesser extent. There were umpteen brands, baby chick No.1, No.2 and No.3, calf pellets and so on. The stock used to come in and had to be checked off from the invoice. The porter signalman loaded it onto the sack barrow and put into the warehouse. We had a terrible job taking stock of the Bibby's: you'd be lost in the warehouse for a day, counting the bags. Sometimes when you got orders in from the agent you found that you hadn't got the stock. So you sent a part order out and waited for a wagon to come in so you could make it up. It was a headache and you had to rely on the men in the shed dishing out the right stuff. Many a time you were ten bags up of one thing and ten bags down of another, as you'd given the wrong stuff out.

Sacks

For many decades until the early 1960s the railway ran a sack hire business. By hiring the empty sacks out to farmers and later conveying them and their contents by rail, a considerable business was built up. Even medium-sized country stations dealt with tens or even hundreds of thousands of sacks each season. During the early summer months, as harvest time drew near, the sacks arrived in wagon loads, in batches of twenty: nineteen sacks inside another sack. The station porters had to deal with the empty sacks when they arrived. There were thousands of sacks in a wagon and they had to be counted and inspected. Some had holes in and had to be sent back to York to be repaired. The hire charge was worked out per sack per week and, when a farmer rented several thousands, the record keeping and accountancy became daunting. It was a task that many railway staff disliked, a few dreaded but at which some became expert. A railway sack would hold 12 stones of oats, 16 stones of barley and wheat or 18 stones of rye. Joe Hatfield found that sacks were a huge business:

The combine harvester was introduced into Ryedale at about the time of my arrival at Helmsley in 1953. They wanted huge quantities of sacks and we stored 200,000 sacks before the beginning of each year's harvest. Farmers used to come along and orders were taken for a thousand, fifteen hundred, two thousand. There were some huge farms in the Nunnington area. The corn was loaded in sacks into vanfits to corn merchants like Kenneth Wilson's and Yorkshire Farmers. I've known people come for sacks at 10 or 11 o'clock at night.

Accounting for the sacks was a tedious job. Every sack that went out had to be recorded as going out and coming back. Demurrage had to be paid after a week and, if a farmer had some grain standing in sacks on his farm, he would have a lot to pay; many were reluctant to do so. Betty Watson seemed to do sacks for most of her working life: 'at Helmsley every market day I used to go up to the market, looking for the farmers, rounding them up to get their accounts paid. I used to spend Fridays in the market place, round the Feversham memorial. I used to see them as I walked round and I would say "now Mr... don't you think you ought to pay the bill?" The majority of them were pretty good, most of them paid'.

Laurie Jackson, a relief clerk, was known as a specialist in sacks, able to sort anyone's problem out. He would be working at Pickering one day and write stern letters to Kirbymoorside, telling them to get the sacks sorted out, when he would be told to go to Kirbymoorside to sort the sacks there out. So he would have to answer his own letter.

Railway sacks were regarded as superior to those of the competition, represented in the locality by a company based at Hovingham: Fox's. The railway sacks were thick and heavy; they could be left in a field overnight and the dew would not soak through to the contents. Fox's sacks, on the other hand, were said to be thin and light and tended to split if dropped. If a farmer found one in a bundle he usually returned it and demanded a swap.

Timber

At several Ryedale stations, timber was a major item. For very many years timber merchants worked in the Helmsley station yard. Roy Andrew was a clerk there from 1918 to 1920 and again from 1940 to 1944: 'timber dominated everything. When I arrived in 1918 one gang of timber loaders was continuously employed there loading long timber, and another gang occasionally at the end of the light railway to Waterloo plantation. Smaller pieces for use as pit-props were loaded daily and forwarded to several coal mines, both from the light railway and the station'. (The light railway into Duncombe Park is described in Chapter 8.) There was an upsurge in 1954 when the station was used to store ship-loads of sawn timber imported at Hull. Helmsley had the space for temporary storage and dockers came from Hull every morning to unload the wagons. Stacks of sawn timber lined the drive to the station and the yard until it went out again.

Timber is remembered at most stations as coming in as 'round timber' – straight from being cut down. During the First World War a tremendous amount of felling went on around Helmsley. Tom Thackray, the son of the Gilling station master, was told that: 'whatever had wheels was pressed into service to bring timber down the road from around Bungdale Head and Scawton, which is the A170 now, to Helmsley station and it became simply an avenue of ruts. It is said that the carts were loaded to such an extent that they wouldn't stand the load and the whole length of the road was apparently punctuated with broken-down vehicles'.

John Lumley recalled that round timber was brought into Sinnington on wood 'cants': 'there were the front wheels and the back wheels, which were attached to a pole with holes through. They could space the wheels to whatever length they wanted, according to how long the timber was. It wasn't a pole wagon as we used to call it, like they used to use on the Wolds. A pole wagon was one where there were two horses on each side of a single shaft'.

It was seldom that station's goods yards were photographed, compared with their platforms and signal boxes. This is Helmsley, with the goods warehouse in the centre and the store for animal feeding stuffs on the left. The station building is on the right. (Author)

Amotherby's small goods yard shortly after closure in 1964. The coal depot is on the left and the BATA mill is on the right. (Author)

Reg Sleightholme, also at Sinnington: 'the timber was dumped in the yard until there was enough to send away. Periodically, when they had got enough, they had a loading session. A rail-mounted crane had been brought earlier by the pickup in readiness, and a timber loading gang came from Malton or York'. Jim Eddon was a timber loader from 1946 or 1947:

There were three in a gang. The foreman measured the length of the tree in feet and 'quarter girthed' it. It was a tape that went round the timber and it was marked in different ways. He had a sheet that had been taken out of a book in the office and he worked out the weight. Some of the timber was loaded onto quints [five flat wagons coupled together] and, if there was an overhang, you put a tail wagon at the end.

Hundreds of tons of larch came from the Newburgh estate into Coxwold station, where it was made into a huge pile in the yard. According to Bob Miller: 'things would be very busy for, say, two years and then there would be a lapse of six months and they would come back again'. Timber was also handled in quantity at Ampleforth from around Yearsley, at Gilling from the woods at Gilling Castle and The Avenue, at Hovingham from the Worsley Estate, and at Slingsby from Castle Howard.

Stone

Limestone from quarries on the M&D travelled via the T&M to Thirsk and on to the blast furnaces at South Bank and Redcar. Burdale quarry was closed in 1955 and Wharram had ceased some time before. As that flow ceased others took its place, notably Thornton Dale on the remaining stub of the closed Pickering to Seamer branch, and Hovingham.

In about 1950 Wath Quarry, just outside Hovingham, started operation, and the stone all went by rail. In these first years the Burdale stone trains – known as 'chalkies' - were still running. Sometimes these trains called at Hovingham to pick wagons up but for most of the time Hovingham had its own train, sometimes two, even three. The stone from Thornton Dale came along the T&M too, often picking up more wagons at Hovingham.

Eric Hartley, Hovingham's porter signalman from 1951 until closure, was very proud of the fact that, because of the stone traffic, latterly his station's monetary takings exceeded the whole of the rest of the T&M and G&P branches; the 44,404 tons of stone despatched in 1958 were considerably more than the total goods tonnage at all the other stations:

We could send fifty wagons of crushed limestone loads in a day, sometimes as many as three trains. In a week we could deal with somewhere between 200 and 250 wagons. We could get a hundred-odd wagons in the station. In the main the empty wagons came from Malton and they were backed in to the long siding; you could get about thirty or a few more down there. And you could get about fifteen up on the coal depot. We would also take so many empty wagons off the train when it came back from Thirsk and we would put them into the yard, anywhere where we had spare room. We had to keep enough room to manoeuvre the wagons about and it was quite an art to get the full and empty wagons in the right place for working the traffic. You soon upset things if you got a relief chap in who didn't know the way it was worked.

You could get about three wagons in the loading dock, but they were moved as soon as they were filled. There was a chap there whose job was to move the wagons along. His name was Paul and he was employed by the quarry.

The method of making steel changed and limestone was no longer needed for lining the furnaces. In 1959 the tonnage fell to 19,815; by 1960 the traffic had virtually ceased. The last train of stone to Thirsk ran on 3 February 1962. There was a short-lived flow of burned limestone, but that finished a few months before the T&M was closed in August 1964.

Photographs of fully-loaded trains of stone - 'chalkies' - are rare. This was taken close to Ampleforth station during the Second World War. The Teesside-bound train has 29 wagons and is hauled by Class J27 No. 891. (Robin Atthill)

15 - Gatehouses and Cottages

As the rail network expanded the increasing numbers of workers who were involved with the day-to-day operation of the railway - porters, platelayers, signalmen and gatekeepers - needed to be housed. Most were platelayers and had to live close to their work. Their accommodation needs were partially fulfilled by the level crossing gatehouses but, where there were insufficient such dwellings, houses were specially provided. On the Ryedale lines there was a mix of both types.

Some gatehouses consisted of two dwellings in the one building, where the gatehouse proper accommodated a husband-and-wife couple, the husband being a platelayer and his wife the gatekeeper. In return for her carrying out the unpaid crossing duties, the house was occupied rent-free. In practice, the gatekeeper performed the duties while her husband was at work; at other times the duties were shared. In later years the wife was paid for her gatekeeping duties but rent was then also charged for the house. The adjacent cottage housed a platelayer. There were 20 such dwellings on the T&M and 22 on the G&P.

Thirsk and Malton

The level crossing gatehouses had only one storey, whereas those elsewhere had two storeys. The number of dwellings is given in brackets:
Gatehouses: Sunbeck (1), Coxwold (2), Cawton (2), Fryton (1), Slingsby (also known as Crabtree Lane) (1), Appleton (1), Swinton (1), Broughton (1), Pasture Lane (also known as Haydon Gate) (1), Pye Pits (1).
Cottages: Thormanby (2), Ampleforth (2), Gilling (4).
All the dwellings on the T&M were built of brick.

Gilling and Pickering

All the dwellings had two storeys.
Gatehouses: Harome (4), Pockley (2), Nawton (2), Starfitt Lane (2), Malton Road (1), Catter Bridge (2), Aislaby Carr (1), Costa Beck (2), Westgate Carr (1), Goslip Bridge (also known as Mill Lane Gate) (2).
Cottages: Kirby Mills (1), Sinnington (2).

The building materials used depended on when construction was undertaken. At Harome, opened with the Gilling and Helmsley branch in 1871, there were four dwellings in two buildings, both of brick. Pockley, Nawton and Starfitt Lane, opened with the Helmsley and Kirbymoorside line in 1874, were all of rock-faced stone. The seven opened with the Kirbymoorside to Pickering line in 1875 used a mixture of materials: Kirby Mills and Malton Road – brick; Catter Bridge and Sinnington – rock-faced stone; Aislaby Carr, Costa Beck, Westgate Carr and Goslip Bridge – ashlar sandstone.

Sunbeck gatehouse was perhaps typical of those on the T&M. The one external door led into the large combined living room and kitchen, off which there was a small pantry. There were two bedrooms. Another room was a bedroom or a sitting room depending on the number of occupants of the house. Apart from the living room and pantry which had a flagstone floor, the rooms had wooden floors, and all the windows of the house had external wooden shutters. Water was pumped from a well outside, said to be over 50 feet deep. The washhouse, which contained a copper, was a sleeper building at the back. At the other side there was the coal house, with an adjacent shed containing the Elsan toilet. The 'stick house', which contained wood for the copper, the kitchen range and the bedroom fires, was nearby. The pigsties were at the back too. The narrow swathe of land on the T&M that had been intended for the never-built second track was cultivated, as also by other tenants of the lineside cottages. The family of Dorothy Hutchinson (née Whincup) lived there from 1928. For Dorothy, who lived there in her formative years, it was a happy place:

It was a lovely place to live because the house was large and the rooms were large. There was an oak fireplace in every one. Along the track, inside the railway fence, my father cultivated the land and we grew blackcurrants, redcurrants and gooseberries. In all there would have been more than an acre of land and it was like a little market garden. He sold plants, both flowers and vegetables, cauliflowers for example at 6d a score. We took the produce on the bicycle to the shop at Raskelf. People used to come from the Pilmoor cottages, from Raskelf and from farms for cauliflower plants. We didn't really know anything but work with my parents. Even when I started to work for a living I used to come home and we pulled the runner beans.

Each crossing was equipped with a 'rotating board signal', also known as a target board, with an iron handle to turn it. To light the lamp there was a short ladder up to a small platform. A 'repeater' bell enabled the block signals that were exchanged between the signal boxes on each side to be heard, but bell signals could not be sent. Margaret Thrower was the gatekeeper at Cawton from summer 1947 until the T&M was closed in 1964:

We were on a 7-to-5 basis, opening at about 7ish. When the signal boxes at Hovingham and Gilling opened in the morning you could hear the bell signals, 5-5-5. The first stone train came at about half past seven. There would be another stone train at about 9 o'clock. Then you would have a break, in between then and a quarter to eleven, when the pickup came. After the pickup you had the first stone train coming back and the second one coming back. If it was very busy you would have an extra stone train and that wouldn't come back until four o'clock. When all the Scarborough trains ran, we were busy. With a bit of luck, when the last stone train came down, the signal boxes would close up and you knew that there would be no more trains. During the day the normal position for the crossing gates was across the road. As soon as you finished at night you opened the gates for the road.

In the meantime the little ones had to be got up and bathed, seen to and fed. I had a board across the bottom of the door, to keep them in. The road was quite busy and every time a car came I had to tootle out and climb over the board to open the gates. The bell was once struck by lightning. It was a lovely day and at about half past one, when I was ironing and had the children playing around me, it just cracked out with thunder. The box was blown clean off the wall and over to the other side of the table. For a while we didn't know when the trains were coming.

You used to hear the bell signal when a train was being offered by Hovingham to Gilling, or vice versa, and then you got a 2 when it was entering the section. When the train came from Hovingham, if it was a clear day you could see the smoke as it was chuffing up behind the wood. For the big stone trains it was a heck of a pull out of Hovingham and it took quite a while. Sometimes car drivers got a bit impatient if they could see that the stone train was only crawling and it was still down behind the wood, and so you had plenty of time to get them over the crossing.

Not all such crossings were hives of activity. As a relief porter, Don Watson worked for three months at Harome gates: 'what a job that was. I started at about half past seven in the morning for the first train, and had to stay until half past seven at night. The gates were kept open for the trains and there was no lunch break because you had to be there in case anybody wanted to go over the crossing. But it only went to some fields and only about twice a week did somebody want to go across. You had to sit there in this cabin and try to find something to do.'

Thirsk and Malton

Right: Coxwold Gates, a short distance west of the station, visible in the background right. (Author)

Below: V2 No. 60924 passing Sunbeck gatehouse on the 10.50 a.m. Scarborough - Newcastle on Saturday, 18 August 1962. The gatehouse is typical of those on the T&M. (Mike Mitchell)

Above: Appleton crossing in August 1962, looking west. A hut for the relief crossing keeper is on the left. The swathe of land for the never-required doubling of the T&M can be seen. At gatehouses it was used as a long, narrow extension to the garden. (Jim Sedgwick)

Left: Pye Pits gatehouse, previously the site of a siding for a limestone quarry, looking east towards Malton in August 1962. (Jim Sedgwick)

Gilling and Pickering

*Pockley Gates, with the guard of the pickup, Sydney Wood, closing the gates behind the train in July 1964. By this time the gatehouses on the G&P were manned only for the very few passenger trains.
(Author's Collection)*

Starfitt Lane gatehouse in the winter following closure. Visible in this photograph, as in those of Pockley Gates and Goslip Bridge, is the bay window nearest to the crossing, so that the crossing keeper could see down the line. The hut for the relief keeper is next to the far gate. (Author)

Left: The Kirbymoorside pickup approaching Starfitt Lane on 24 July 1957 behind J39 No. 64867. Kirkdale viaduct is in the distance. (Jim Sedgwick)

Below: Westgate Carr gatehouse looking west in 1953, at about the time of the closure of this section of line. (J.W. Armstrong Trust)

Goslip Bridge gatehouse in November 1956, three years after the track had been lifted. The then still-open line from Rillington to Whitby can be seen in the background. (Jim Sedgwick)

16 - Track and Maintenance

When the track on T&M was opened in 1853 it had rails fifteen feet long weighing 65lbs. per yard. There were five sleepers per rail, unevenly spaced. The same 65-lb rail was still in use on the T&M in 1871, when the line from Gilling to Helmsley was opened. As Captain Tyler, the Board of Trade Inspector, walked the new line east of Gilling and alongside the T&M, he observed that the latter was in an unsatisfactory condition and should, he reported, be replaced. The Gilling to Helmsley branch had rails 24 feet long, 82lb per yard. The sleepers were of creosoted scotch fir, nine feet long by ten inches by five inches, 2 ft 8 in apart. The ballast was of coke refuse, one foot deep below the undersides of the sleepers. The extensions to Kirbymoorside in 1874 and Pickering in 1875 were probably the same. It is probable too that standard 95lb bullhead rail was eventually used throughout, variously in 24-foot, 30-foot and 60-foot lengths.

The maintenance system divided rail routes into lengths, each maintained by a small gang of from three to five men, consisting of a ganger and lengthmen. In rural areas, especially on single lines, the optimum distance for a length depended on the how far it was possible for a gang to walk during the course of a working day *and* carry out the requisite maintenance. In 1867 T.E. Harrison referred to T&M as an example: '[it] is laid nearly on the surface, the works being light, gradients easy, ballast good, and traffic small, [and] is well maintained by the labour of three men to every four miles of line (0.75 men per mile)...' Given that the combined railways of Ryedale were 41 miles long, this equates to 30 men.

The track maintenance men may have walked to their places of work but Wilfred Jackson, whose home was at Cawton gatehouse, remembered man-powered trolleys being used. This is confirmed by the 'novel and exciting race' that took place during the mid-1880s, during the 36-year tenure of Gilling's first station master, Mr Wright, on the two parallel single lines of the T&M and G&P east of the station. An anonymous newspaper has the details:

A race took place on Saturday evening at Gilling station on the North Eastern Railway between two bogies built to run on the line. The older machine was designed by the station master at Gilling thirty years ago, and is a model of simplicity in its principle and construction. It consists of two hind wheels about three feet diameter, with cranked axle, driven by a pair of treadles, and brake for stopping; the two leading wheels are little more than half the diameter of the other. It is constructed to carry six.

The other is a new machine built in the North Eastern Railway permanent way shops at York on a somewhat novel and showy principle. It was constructed to carry four, two of which worked the machine, but is now altered, all four having treadles and take part in propelling. It has two large wheels a little under three feet diameter, and two smaller of about two feet diameter, with double action brake applying to the wheels; the machinery is somewhat extensive and complicated; four pairs of treadles apply to a cranked shaft on which are two cog wheels and chains connecting with similar wheels on the axle of the larger running wheels.

In the test race, the old machine was placed on the Gilling and Pickering branch line, and the new one on the Thirsk and Malton (the two lines run parallel for a mile and three-quarters). The old machine carried one worker and two others, and the new machine carried four, all workers. The lines decline slightly from the starting point, and the wind was favourable.

The new machine got off first, and took the lead by eight or ten yards for a short distance, but the old machine gradually gained, and passed the opponent in the first quarter mile, and so continued to gain during the remainder of the distance, arriving at the finishing point one minute fifteen seconds in advance of the new machine. The highest rate of speed attained by the old machine was fifteen miles per hour. A looker on, who has travelled in America and has seen several of their machines of this kind, says the old machine 'is the best he has seen, and it ought to have been patented twenty years ago'.

In the late 1920s 55 men were employed collectively on the Ryedale lines and on the Seamer to Pickering branch. In 1930 the York District of the LNER introduced what turned out to be a revolution in track maintenance on (mostly) rural single- and double-track lines. Small gangs of platelayers covering short distances were replaced by large gangs that covered greater areas. The members of these gangs moved about their territories by means of petrol-driven rail trolleys, later known as Engineer's Rail Motors (ERMs). The first line to be so changed was the Nidd Valley branch to Pateley Bridge in 1930. By the end of 1932 the York District had introduced similar schemes utilising 190 motor trolleys with an estimated annual saving of £33,725. By the end of 1933 185 rail motors were in use in the North East Area of the LNER, producing a saving of 355 track maintenance men. Moreover 'in spite of this reduction in staff, the standard of maintenance has not only been maintained, but considerably improved in a great many cases'.

An Engineer's Rail Motor on the G&P from Helmsley and passing the Gilling up distant signal, viewed from a pickup on the T&M on 5 August 1964. (Author)

The members of the larger gangs continued to live in the original lineside cottages. They proceeded by ERM to the daily site of their work, which might be several miles away. However, introducing the ERMs was one thing; optimising the gangs' new mobility was another. On single lines the Electric Tablet and Electric Key Token systems, described in Chapter 10, ensured that only one train or vehicle was in a block section at any one time. It would have made the new equipment less than useful if, every time a train came along the line, the ERM had to run to the nearest station or siding to be taken out of the way. Their introduction was therefore accompanied by the creation of 'occupation posts', known unofficially as 'run-offs', very short pieces of track at right angles to the rail line, approximately one to one-and-a-half miles apart. A small turntable that was an integral part of the ERM enabled it to be rotated, removed from the line and onto the run-off.

The run-offs were equipped with a connection into the block system. When an ERM entered a section it was not given a tablet, but instead a 'key and plug': a flex with a key at one end and a plug at the other. Withdrawal of the key and plug from the signal box locked the block system and prevented the withdrawal of a tablet. The LNER Magazine of June 1932 explained the routine:

The key-plug combination is the token which is given to the ganger. When the ganger arrives at one of the occupation points he removes the rail motor car from the running line, inserts the key in the key box forming part of the car equipment and connects the trolley to the occupation point by means of the flexible cable, inserting the four-point plug at one end into the socket on the trolley key box and the plug at the other end into a box fitted on a post on the occupation point. He is then in a position to telephone the signal box or boxes concerned by means of a telephone attached to the car. The inserting and locking of the key and plug enables the signalman to clear his switch instrument and restore normal token working.

The length of the flex was enough to reach between the post and the ERM when the latter was on the run-off. When the ERM was put back onto the line, the key and plug was disconnected, which once again locked the block system until it was plugged in again or had returned to the station. At the end of a day's work it was usually left in a garage in a siding or at a run-off. A trailer could also be conveyed.

1933 saw the Electric systems introduced on the last part of the G&P, so as to facilitate the introduction of the ERMs, which was done in June that year. There were 54 run-offs in total, about one per mile, on the Ryedale lines and the Seamer to Pickering branch. After the introduction of the ERMs the maintenance of these lines was subsequently carried out by 36 men, a saving of 19. The estimated cost for 11 trolleys and three trailers, including shelters, electrical equipment, *etc.* was £5,653 but a net annual saving of £1,545 was anticipated.

Even with the introduction of the more mobile gangs, there was still the task of regularly inspecting the track, carried out by a 'track-walker' who covered up to 12 miles of line. For many years Tom Whincup of Sunbeck gatehouse was the track-walker for the western part of T&M. He was one of those countrymen to whom walking his length each day brought freedom, and for whom the attractions of promotion were limited. His daughter, Dorothy Hutchinson, recalls his working days:

He covered the line from Sunbeck eastwards as far as Gilling, ten miles away, every day. Sometimes he walked to Gilling and rode the train back; at other times he rode the train to Gilling and walked back. Sometimes I went with him as far as Husthwaite

Gate. He would carry on to Gilling, either walking or on the train depending on which he was doing, and he would pick me up on the way back. He took with him a 'Scarborough bucket' - that is a small one like you take to the seaside - and in that he carried things like staples which he put into the sleepers if they needed replacing, to let the gang know.

Archie Greenley, who lived in one of the Harome cottages with his family, was another track walker some years later:

My headquarters was in the gate cabin at Harome, where my hammer was kept, with the spare keys for the rails and oil for the points. Each morning I walked to Helmsley, knocking the keys in. Then I caught the passenger train from Helmsley to Gilling. I worked up towards Coxwold for a mile, came back and did the yard at Gilling, oiling the points in the yard. Then I had my dinner and set sail back to Harome, checking the keys as I came. I had the nearly two miles of double track and another mile towards Hovingham. We had a plant called Stone Crop growing on the line for about a mile near Gilling. We used to call it the Golden Mile; once you get it you can't get rid of it.

In very hot weather if I saw a buckle in the line, I had to loosen the nuts in the fish plates, so that the rail could retract. A train would push the track out. Then I had to tighten the nuts up again. I had to see to any gaps in the fences, in case cattle and sheep got onto the line. I repaired them temporarily until the gang came out to repair them properly.

The track walkers also had to check the bridges and viaducts. Archie Greenley kept an eye on the Rye Bridge: 'I used to look over the top and, if I saw a crack, I used to get down and have a look'. Similarly Tom Magson, between Helmsley and Pickering, looked at Kirkdale Viaduct: 'we would go down to the ground under the viaduct and have a look up at the arches. They used to crumble a bit underneath inside the arches, which were made of brick. They used to send stonemasons out from York'.

A contented man: Tom Whincup, track walker from 1928 until his death in 1963, standing in August 1962 outside his home, Sunbeck gatehouse. (Mike Mitchell)

The permanent way maintenance gang at the Costa Beck run-off during the late 1940s. Left to right: Cyril Magson, Ted Tate, Albert Watson (father), Bob Atkinson, Ernest Watson (son), Tom Magson, George Thorpe. (Courtesy Ernest Watson)

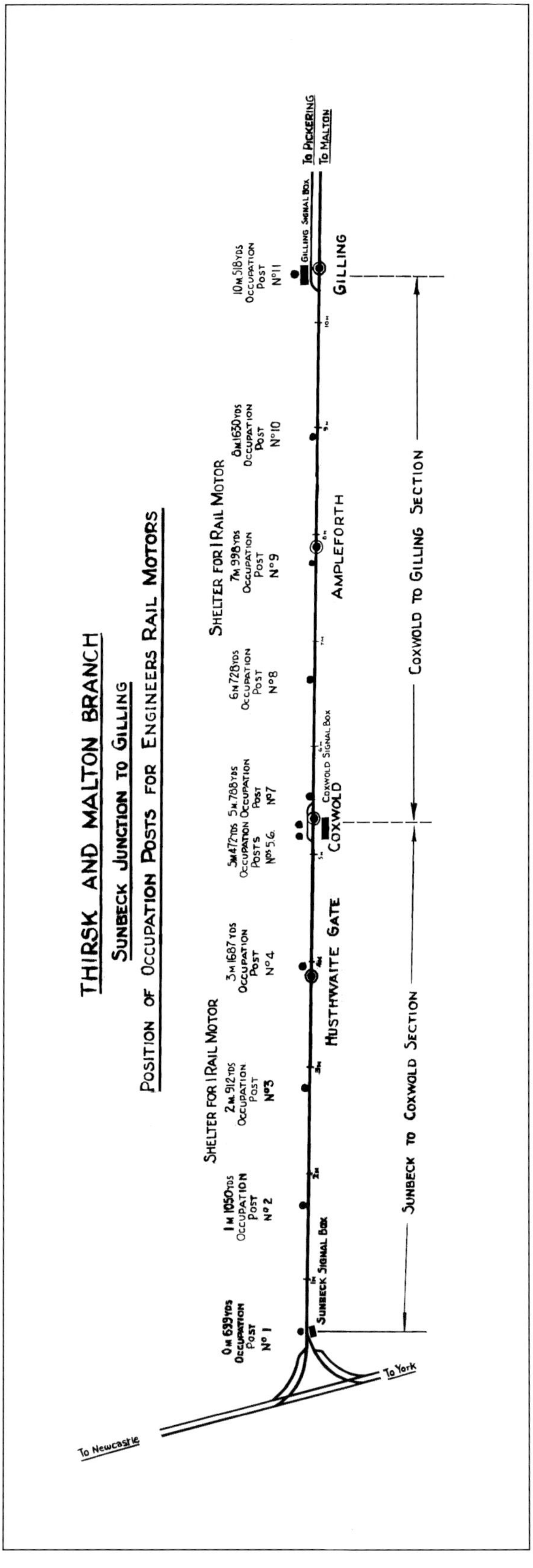

THIRSK AND MALTON BRANCH
SUNBECK JUNCTION TO GILLING
POSITION OF OCCUPATION POSTS FOR ENGINEERS RAIL MOTORS

Occupation Posts (Sunbeck Junction to Gilling):
- 0m 639yds Occupation Post No. 1 — Sunbeck Signal Box
- 1m 1050yds Occupation Post No. 2
- 2m 912yds Occupation Post No. 3 — Shelter for 1 Rail Motor
- 3m 1687yds Occupation Post No. 4 — Husthwaite Gate
- 5m 177yds / 5m 708yds Occupation Posts Nos. 5 & 6 — Coxwold Signal Box, Coxwold
- 6m 728yds Occupation Post No. 7
- 7m 998yds Occupation Post No. 8 — Ampleforth
- 8m 1650yds Occupation Post No. 9 — Shelter for 1 Rail Motor
- 10m 518yds Occupation Post No. 10 — Gilling Signal Box, Gilling
- No. 11 — To Pickering / To Malton

Sections: Sunbeck to Coxwold Section; Coxwold to Gilling Section

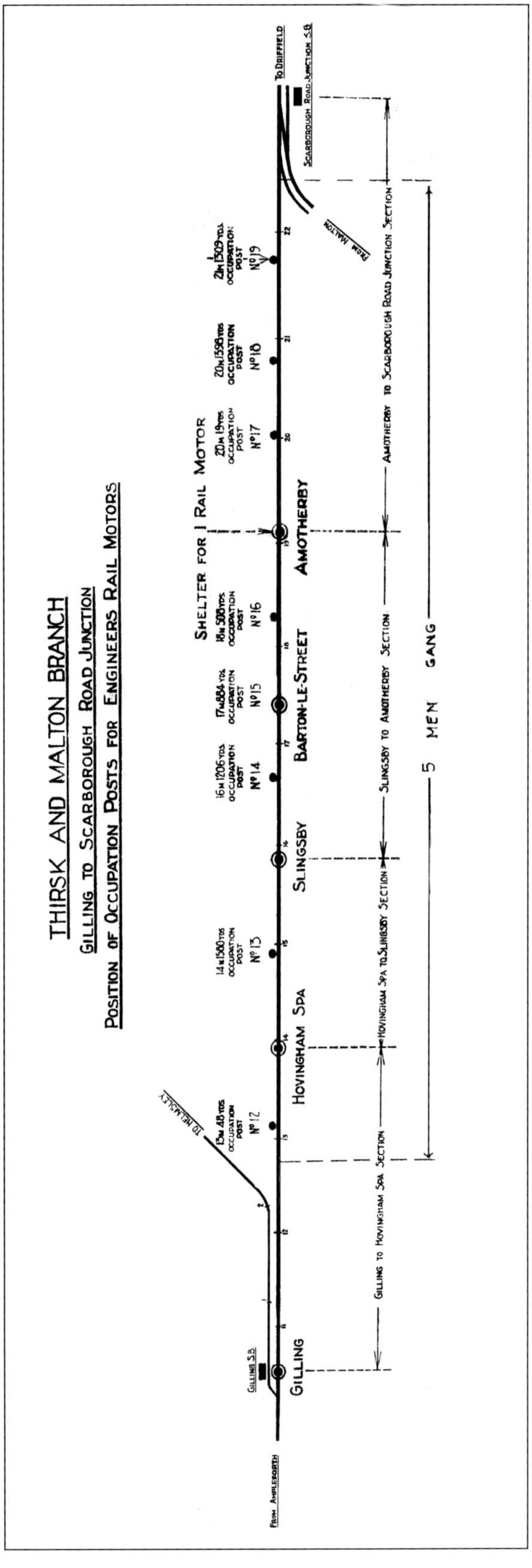

To Newcastle / To York

THIRSK AND MALTON BRANCH
GILLING TO SCARBOROUGH ROAD JUNCTION
POSITION OF OCCUPATION POSTS FOR ENGINEERS RAIL MOTORS

From Ampleforth — Gilling S.B. — Gilling
- 13m 45yds Occupation Post No. 12 — To Pilmoor (?)
- 14m 1500yds Occupation Post No. 13 — Hovingham Spa
- 16m 1206yds Occupation Post No. 14 — Slingsby
- 17m 884yds Occupation Post No. 15 — Barton-le-Street
- 18m 500yds Occupation Post No. 16 — Shelter for 1 Rail Motor
- 19m — Amotherby
- 20m 19yds Occupation Post No. 17
- 20m 1598yds Occupation Post No. 18
- 21m 509yds Occupation Post No. 19 — Scarborough Road Junction S.B. — From Malton — To Driffield

Sections: Gilling to Hovingham Spa Section; Hovingham Spa to Slingsby Section; Slingsby to Amotherby Section; Amotherby to Scarborough Road Junction Section

5 MEN GANG

17 - The Second World War

In 1940, soon after the start of the War, Frank Hick, a York District Traffic Inspector, visited the Ryedale stations: 'I had to draw a rough plan of each and every station and say if they had an end dock and, if there wasn't one, what the prospects were of making one, quickly. And the location in relation to the Moors and villages and everything associated with the wartime effort'. As a result Helmsley was chosen as a suitable station for the transhipment of tanks. The open, uncultivated North York Moors were ideal for tank warfare training.

A successful test move was carried out in August 1941, involving a part of the 30th Armoured Brigade. Five 'Armoured Fighting Vehicle' trains were sent from Grosmont to Helmsley, and three personnel and baggage trains from Whitby to Helmsley. The Army pronounced the railway arrangements 'admirable'. At the end of June 1943 the Guards Armoured Division – the 2nd Battalion Grenadier Guards, 1st Coldstream Guards, 2nd Irish Guards and 2nd Welsh Guards - arrived at Helmsley. The first three had just been armed with U.S. Sherman tanks and the Welsh Guards had British Cromwell tanks. As many as 24 trains of tanks, possibly more, arrived at Helmsley between June and September. The headquarters was at Duncombe Park and the troops lived in huts. Ernest Leaman, Helmsley's station master from 1943 recalled that:

We had tank trains every week, two or three sometimes. On a tank train there were nine 'warflats', a store wagon, a guard's van and one coach for the tank crews. The Cromwell tank was slightly wider than the warflat and it had to be positioned very exactly, so that four or five inches on either side stuck out, no more. We nearly always had to load them in the evening, which was all right in summer time. In winter when it was dark the soldiers used to stand, one on either side, and smoke cigarettes. The glow from the cigarettes was used by the driver to guide the tank. The drivers had to be very, very careful.

Roy Andrew, Helmsley's chief clerk, remembered a young driver who had never previously driven a tank along the full length of a train and it toppled over the side:

There was pandemonium and nobody knew how to retrieve this situation. They had conferences and got piles of sleepers to put underneath the tracks, but these got ground up when they tried to move the tank. I was talking to an old county council road foreman, who knew how to get it back on. 'There's all these tanks about here,' he said 'and they've all got wire ropes. They get one tank at one side and fix a wire rope to the track that's on the wagon; another on the side that's on the ground. The one with the rope on the track that's on the wagon pulls while the other one holds it steady. It'll get to a position clear of the wagon, they take the wagon away and gently let the tank down again.' So I went up to a Major and I said 'go and ask that old man over there. He'll put you right. He's just told me how to put it on.' The tank was on in about 20 minutes.

The Rt. Hon. Robert Boscawen M.C., then a young officer in the 1st Battalion Coldstream Guards, has written that 'our Sherman tanks were higher above the ground than the Cromwells, so that the warflats had to be deeper in the middle. This made driving the tanks onto them even more tricky and I seem to remember that they were loaded one by one and the train was fitted together afterwards. Certainly one or two tanks fell off the side with a loud bang I recall, but an ingenious REME officer, I think, found a way of moving the warflat alongside the sloping end of the passenger platform so that the driver could drive off the warflat onto the platform'.

The Guards Armoured Division departed for tented camps on the Wolds near Driffield in late 1943, and later fought in northern France and at Arnhem. They were replaced at Helmsley by the Rocky Mountain Rangers, from Kamloops, Canada, who were later remembered for their bands. Roy Andrew:

If they knew that one of their own troop trains was coming, they would send a band down, sometimes two bands, and they'd play outside the goods office. There was pandemonium, and if there were two bands one conductor would be waiting for the other to finish, with no pause in the music. I came to work one morning and when I went into the office the station master seemed to be very grumpy. I said 'what's wrong?' 'what's wrong? Damned Rocky Mountain Rangers! At half past three this morning, they were blasting away outside my bedroom window. I finally got them to stop and I said "What are you doing?" "We've come to meet the troops" "You're on the wrong day. They're not coming until tomorrow!"' Then he said to me 'I've got to face that again tomorrow!'

The Royal Train carrying King George VI, Queen Elizabeth and Princess Elizabeth came to Helmsley on 22 March 1944. Earnest Leaman had his own role to play: 'I had to receive the King; my Superintendent at York was on the Royal Train and he turned round to me and said "you've got to receive him. You're the station master". The Major-General commanding the Division introduced me'. The Prime Minister, Mr Churchill, also came on two occasions. Roy Andrew: 'one time when he was coming, the dogs were barking it all over Helmsley that he was coming the following day. We'd heard nothing officially about it. We'd got a telegram, asking us to provide five pints of milk for a special train arriving at such-and-such a time. The General Officer Commanding and all his cohorts arrived that morning to find out the exact time of the train that was bringing the Prime Minister and they came in: "Now station master, could you tell us the time of the train the Prime Minister is coming on?" "Prime Minister? No, I don't know." "Surely you know by now. He should be coming very soon." "No, I've heard nothing official at all. I'll tell you what I have received. I've received a telegram asking me to provide five pints of milk for a special train arriving at 11.30 a.m. Don't tell me Mr Churchill has started drinking milk, because I won't believe it." That was the only intimation we actually had about it'. On the train's way back from Helmsley the clerk at Gilling, Arthur Gillery, was charged with making arrangements for Churchill to 'get a copy of the *Yorkshire Evening Press*. It was all arranged, and the *Press* duly arrived from York. As the train came through Gilling it was going pretty fast, despite the tablet change, and someone else was looking for the guard to give him the paper, but there was no-one on the train to take it. So after all that trouble Churchill didn't get his *Press*'.

An airfield was built at Wombleton, in the middle of Ryedale and close to both Nunnington and Nawton stations. It was used by 1666 Heavy Conversion Unit, part of 6 Group Bomber Command, whose role was to convert air crew to flying heavier types of aircraft. Construction commenced early in 1943. From April until September 30 or more trains of stone and slag were taken to Nunnington station and their contents conveyed to the airfield site. The slag, from the Teesside steelworks, made a good foundation for the runways. Nunnington station was very busy as a result, with two extra men working there for the six months of the building work. To move the wagons about the yard a small steam shunting engine was brought in. Rita Jackson, whose father Tom Atkinson was in charge of Nunnington station at the time, remembered that the driver's name was Steve and he lived in the station house: 'he was only a little man and was always covered in oil'. The identity of the engine is unknown.

Ammunition and stores came in and went out by rail through many stations, including Ampleforth, Gilling, Slingsby, Amotherby and Kirbymoorside. A girl then, Margaret Thrower lived in one of the lineside cottages at Cawton: 'you had ammunition trains during the night. You used to think the house was tumbling down, when it was dark and one of those long ammunition trains was going by. Not knowing when they were coming didn't help. You were asleep and then suddenly awake as these trains trundled by. They were only moving slowly and it was terrifying for a young girl'.

At Gilling a special siding was installed into a field next to the goods yard. At Slingsby a large concrete apron was laid alongside the existing siding parallel to the main line. Fred Wright of Slingsby: 'sometimes about a hundred wagons would come in a day. Two or three hundred soldiers unloaded them and took the ammunition away in lorries to the woods on the Castle Howard estate. One day when an ammunition train was in, we were in the house and a man put his head in the window and said "hold your hat on; one of the wagons is on fire!" I said "shall we get under the table, or what?" He replied "it won't make any difference as it'll just blow everything up." We got every bucket and everything we could think of and they came into our back yard and passed water from one man to the next, until the fire was out'. The ammunition was dispersed into the countryside along the sides of country roads, behind hedges and in woodlands.

George Kettlewell, station master at Ampleforth, had a lot of petrol, ammunition and stores. About half an hour before the first train was due, a 2nd Lieutenant, a sergeant and a private from the Movement Control arrived:

They said 'you're not used to much traffic here, are you?' I said 'no', so they said 'we'll show you what to do and then you'll just want us an odd time again afterwards.' I said 'that's very kind of you.' They didn't know how to release the points and I had to show them that. It was rather an awkward yard as we could only get in with about eight wagons and then the engine had to come out again. They hadn't a clue and asked me what to do. I said 'you've come to show me'. About an hour later the engine driver got fed up and went up to the 2nd Lieutenant and he said 'look, there's your car across there. Bloody well get into it and clear off.' We never saw them again. He and the guard soon had it straightened out.

When the Pioneers first started they handled shells as though they were eggs, but it wasn't long before they were throwing them one to the other, everything except detonators. We used to get odd wagons of detonators in and we only 'touched' them; they were in a shock wagon and had to be hand braked. You would put them up at the top of the yard and run them down into position. They were rather tricky and had to be handled with care.

One afternoon a through freight train drew up, with a hot box on a petrol tank. He drew forward and backed into the yard with the wagon. Flames were coming out and it didn't look very bright, so my wife and daughter went across to the nearby farm a quarter of a mile away. The heat from the oil had locked the door into the axle box and I couldn't get it off, and so I couldn't get at the oil pad. It looked serious and I rang the Army. They came down with some extinguishers and soon had it out.

Lord Killanin came down one day and said 'I have a salmon on the way from Galway. As soon as it comes in let me know, will you?' Weeks passed and there was no salmon, until one morning the guard opened the door and kicked out a basket. I said 'that's no way to handle a fish.' He said 'no, and if you had to travel with it as far as I have you would have had it out before.' It had been about three weeks on the way and it wasn't eatable. So I rang his Lordship and he brought some staff down and they buried it and gave it the last rites.

Lord Killanin was then Adjutant of the King's Royal Rifle Corps (Queen's Westminsters) in Ampleforth village (and President of the International Olympic Committee from 1972 until 1980). Writing many years later, he had a vague recollection of the incident: 'the salmon was sent from my gamekeeper in Spiddal, Co. Galway, in the far west of Ireland, so even in normal times without any freezing it would not have been very fresh on arrival. I can remember walking down and collecting parcels at Ampleforth station at other times'.

With such a large number of forces personnel in the area there was great demand for the passenger train service. Rene Armstrong noticed that:

We were selling a lot of tickets to Alne, where they would change to go to Scotland. We didn't have printed tickets to Alne so we wrote them out by hand. I began to think there was something fishy so the next Monday morning I examined them carefully when they were handed in. We found that they were made out to Edinburgh, and many other places. One of the men had been buying tickets to Alne, which were very cheap. They used some stuff to rub our writing out, and sold them to friends at a profit, making them out for where they wanted to go to. The same thing happened with return tickets to Gilling. We watched out for the return halves coming back and found that they'd been altered to GillingHAM, in Kent. A man was caught and I had to go up to the court martial, as I had issued the tickets. They sent the car down for me from Duncombe Park and I waited to be called as a witness. He pleaded not guilty so that was one day gone. But then he changed his plea, and I had therefore to go again on another day, and wait to be called as a witness. I went into this long tent, and I was the only female there.

When the soldiers returned, at different times Olive, Betty and I used to be on the gate out of the station. They used to come back with all sorts of odd tickets: tram tickets and bus tickets. It was quite ridiculous really. We couldn't do anything about it as there was such a terrific number of them. They used to jump over the fence and then away into the town. When we got into the office and put them on the table, we found cigarette cards, tram tickets and all sorts.

Olive Wrightson wondered 'what you could do when you had hundreds of soldiers and you just had to stand there by the station entrance?' The matter was reported to the Orderly Room and four military policemen were sent down the following Monday morning. 'We took no end of money but it took ages to get the men through. But that didn't last very long before we went back to the same old thing again.'

Unfortunately, as John Dawson found out, the train service consisted of only two passenger trains per day in each direction, which threatened to curtail weekend leave. He was bound for Nawton and RAF Wombleton:

A train left York at about 2.30 a.m. on the Monday for Scarborough passing through Malton, where it was possible to catch a connection for Pickering. The two coaches for the Scarborough train stood unlocked in Platform 12 at York and it was possible to get in and snatch some sleep before the train set off. Care had to be taken in the dark not to sit on someone already in occupation. We arrived at Pickering an hour or more before the morning train set out. There was usually a substantial gathering of people returning from leave but we were not allowed to board the coaches as the siding had no platform to give access to them. This resulted in a cold wait in a crowded waiting room if you were lucky and a colder one outside if you were not. We arrived at Nawton in good time for us to book in at the guard room by 8 a.m. though it meant going on duty without a great deal of sleep of course.

On Saturdays nights, starting in September 1943, the LNER laid on a special train to take the servicemen from Helmsley and other stations to Scarborough for a night out. These 'recreational' trains left Helmsley at 5 p.m. and Scarborough at 11 p.m., and returned empty to York in the early hours of the Sunday morning.

At 1 a.m. on Sunday 4 March 1945 a Luftwaffe Junkers 88G-6 night fighter fired at two bombers that were coming in to land at RAF Dishforth. On its way back home the German aircraft spotted a moving train, the empty Saturday recreational train, returning from Helmsley to York. Its pilot, Leutnant Arnold Döring, had been instructed not to return with any ammunition, so 'I fired a long burst at a train which let out a lot of steam as I shot it full of holes'. The train had stopped at Gilling to pick up 34-year old Tom Inman, a relief signalman resident at 3 Railway Cottages with his wife Mary. It paused briefly at Coxwold and left there at 1.35 a.m. towards Sunbeck. The train stopped at Sunbeck's home signal where Albert Clemit was on duty:

When the train got to the cabin it stopped. The driver said 'we've been machine gunned up there, and we picked a chap up at Gilling, who's coming to work.' So I went to have a look, as he hadn't got off. I didn't dare use the hand lamp, so I used a torch. The guard came down, we walked along and we got to the first compartment. I shouted but there was no answer. Then I looked inside. The guard said 'has he been hit?' I said 'yes and I think he's dead.' They took him on into York.

According to Bob Miller: 'the train stopped at Coxwold and tipped about two tons of coal off, for the gatehouse and signal box. If it hadn't been for that Tom might not have been killed. Mr Hunsley, the station master, was very shaky about that, for fear that it got out about the train being stopped there'.

Enemy air activity affected the Ryedale lines on several other occasions. Early in the morning of Wednesday 16 April 1941 a bomb fell on the line east of Coxwold. No-one heard the explosion that tore into the track. Moreover, the signal wires were left intact. The first train the next morning, the 7.20 a.m. passenger train from Pickering, was sent from Gilling as normal and fell into the crater. Fred Wright was on duty at Ampleforth: 'Batty [the Coxwold signalman] rang up and said "where's that train? Has he left there yet Fred?" I said "yes, he's been gone about a quarter of an hour." "There must be something wrong" he said, so I said "I'll slip up round the bend and have a look." When I got round the bend the guard was walking back along the line towards me'.

The locomotive was Class D20 4-4-0 2108, driven by Jack Catling, with Fireman Jim Martindale and Guard Joe Hanson. On the train there were several railway employees bound for York, some to attend a day class in railway work. The following is a composite account, provided by Rene Armstrong, Betty Watson, Eric and Olive Wrightson, who were travelling from Helmsley to York:

The engine ended up on its side, half buried in the soft, black soil. The driver had been looking out of his side and as a consequence he didn't see the hole; otherwise he might have stopped in time. We were travelling along quite normally, just talking, and without warning there was this terrific lurch, and the luggage fell off the racks. We were aghast when we got out and saw the big hole. Luckily no-one was injured. Usually the guard travelled at the front of the train but that morning he chose to travel at the rear. That saved his life because the front coach, a parcels van, was concertina-ed. There were two boxes of eggs in there but not one of them was broken. The driver was a very small man and he was able to squeeze through the window in the cab of the engine. We had to walk along the line to Coxwold station. The 7.43 train from York was standing at Coxwold station, waiting for our train to pass it. It couldn't go any further so the engine ran round its train and took us to York.

The line was reopened at 9.30 p.m. Following this incident, whenever airplanes were heard overhead during the night, the line was examined by platelayers on an ERM before the commencement of services the next morning.

There was a near-miss when four bombs straddled Kirbymoorside station on Monday 3 August 1942. Vera Heath (née Watson), Kirbymoorside clerk at the time, was at home: 'it was a lovely day. We had visitors and were washing up after lunch when we heard this plane and went out. Then we saw these things come out of the plane and we didn't stand out there for much longer!' Richard Boddy, a child at the time, was playing in the yard at home: 'It was the Bank Holiday. I looked in the sky at this plane. Then all of a sudden these black things started to come out of it. "Look Dad!" I shouted. You never saw him move so fast, and he grabbed me by the neck and he threw me and my friend to the ground. We waited for the explosion, for the ground to come up and hit us in the stomach, but nothing happened: they didn't go off'. There were four bombs. One fell at the south end of the station bridge, another within 50 feet of Russell's Agricultural Implement works, another at Moorlin a house across from the station, and another nearby. Richard Boddy's father was an ARP warden and went to the scene: 'I remember him saying to me that the bomb had fallen right on the southern end of the bridge and that, if it had gone off, it would have destroyed the station'. As for the bomb that fell at Moorlin, Richard Boddy again: 'when my Dad got there, he found the butler sweeping the lawn with a brush, sweeping the debris back into the hole. The bomb was ticking!' Dorothy Oldfield (née Dobson), the daughter of the station master Herbert Dobson, was at home: 'my father had been watching this German plane flying around and he came in for his tin hat. We had to leave the house in a hurry and they wouldn't let any of us come in until it was safe. It took the bomb disposal people two days to dig the bombs out, and when we went back home there were mouldy pieces of potato on the table'. It was found that all the bombs had been sabotaged, possibly by the forced labourers that had manufactured them in Germany.

Three other incidents caused minor disruption. At 4 a.m. on 14 June 1941 a German plane dropped a string of bombs around the T&M's north curve between Sunbeck and Sessay Wood junction: one in the field, two on the railway and two in another field. Harold Burn and his family at Oak Farm, Pilmoor, found the next morning that 'two bombs had dropped into some potatoes which we had only planted two days before, and they had been dug up!' The line was repaired and pronounced safe for traffic at 6.25 a.m. On 24 July 1943 a high explosive bomb fell close to the line between Helmsley and Nunnington, near Harome Gate's up distant signal. The only damage was a broken rail on the single line. Immediate repairs were made and normal working was resumed at 11.50 a.m.

Lastly on 16 February 1944 a Halifax bomber based at RAF Leconfield, near Beverley, crashed near the line between Sunbeck and Husthwaite Gate between 1.20 and 1.50 a.m. There had been no trains during the night and the signal boxes at Coxwold and Sunbeck were closed. Normal working was resumed at 10.28 a.m. when repairs to the telegraph wires had been carried out.

18 - Locomotives and Train Running

Few country branch lines had as wide a variety of locomotives as the T&M and G&P: from the small tank engine to the powerful Pacific, from the NER BTP 0-4-4T to the streamlined LNER A4 4-6-2. No information exists on the first locomotives to be used from 1853. Moreover there is only a reference to 'a tank engine on the saddle back principle' when the first part of the G&P was opened in 1871. It is possible that this was NER No. 345, a rebuild of a tender engine dating from 1846. Much information on engines in the NER era is available in signal box occurrence books and photographs. The BTP (Bogie Tank Passenger) 0-4-4T engine was the mainstay of the early passenger service. Goods trains were generally in the hands of various types of NER 0-6-0 engine, including Classes 13, 59, 93, 398 and 708. Some of these were occasionally used on excursion trains.

NER Classes A 2-4-2T, B 0-6-2T, O 0-4-4T and U 0-6-2T were also used on passenger trains before the First World War. As G5s, the NER Class Os were used in LNER days. Some of them were later used on 'push-and-pull' trains, which operated the Pickering to Helmsley afternoon school trains in the 1950s. Popular with locomotive crews, the push-and-pull maintained its engine permanently at one end. Sandy Atkinson of Malton shed provides a reminiscence of G5s when they were in use on push-and-pull trains during the 1940s:

The cab at the coach end was very small and had little round windows looking forward. There were usually two coaches but it could take three. At the back there sometimes might be a couple of cattle wagons and a horsebox, so that the engine would have been sandwiched in the middle.

When the driver was in the coach the fireman was left on his own in the loco. Between the cab and the engine there was an electrical jumper cable for bell signals. The driver gave the fireman a 2 bell code, that was his indication to open the steam regulator. As the train started the fireman opened the regulator. The driver had another gauge as well as the brake gauge which told him when the fireman was opening and shutting the regulator. Even if the driver had been deaf he could have seen the regulator being opened or closed. It worked!

Ron Benson, also of Malton shed, also worked the push-and-pulls for three years as a fireman but in his day the procedure was different:

My own engine was a G5, number 505. I used to have it all polished up, brasses and everything. The push-and-pull was easier than a normal engine and was very good. The regulator was controlled by vacuum: when the driver was at the other end, when he shut off with his lever it closed a valve in the engine to cut off steam. Sometimes it didn't close properly and so, to overcome that, we used to put a penny in the pipe so it cut it off altogether. As a result, all the driver did when he was driving from the coach end was use the brake, because as the fireman I did all the opening up and shutting off from the engine. I opened it out and shut off when I thought, notched up and opened out again, gave him more steam. I looked out as we went along and knew when we had to shut off, and the driver just sat there doing the brakes.

On 11 May 1908 one of the NER's two 1903 petrol-electric autocars was used on the York to Pickering service, the first time it was seen in Ryedale. Shortly afterwards, on 1 July that year, they were sent to work the Selby to Cawood service. It is possible that one of these vehicles were used on the Malton to Gilling service, for there is another record of one in 1921 at Slingsby. Between 1924 and 1943 the York/Pickering passenger service passed to Class D20 4-4-0 locomotives. The engine that fell into the bomb crater in April 1941 (see Chapter 17), D20 2108, was repaired and later numbered 62387 by BR. It hauled the Branch Line Society railtour to Kirbymoorside in June 1957.

This is the earliest known photograph of an engine on the Ryedale lines. Only the recognisable figure of Richard Jennings, Kirbymoorside's first station master, on the left indicates that it was taken at that station. No. 491 was an NER Class 59 0-6-0 which, along with other members of the class, regularly hauled the pickup. Of the five central figures standing on the ground, the pair on the left may be clerks. (Author's Collection)

Two of the staple passenger engines on the line in its last decades are seen together at Gilling on 16 July 1949; on the left D20 4-4-0 No. E2369 (later 62369) awaits the arrival of D49 4-4-0 No 62774 The Staintondale possibly on an inspection saloon. (Chris Wilson)

The late 1920s saw the introduction by the LNER of the Sentinel steam rail car, a single coach with built-in steam boiler and engine. They were introduced as the last, unsuccessful, attempt to reduce the cost of running the Malton/Gilling service. 2236 *British Queen* was new in September 1929. Based at Malton it covered 42,176 miles in its first year. 238 *Yorkshire Huzzar* too was used. Their lower parts were painted green and the upper parts cream. Each one could also pull a trailer, either an extra coach, also painted green and cream, or a horse box. The seats were reversible.

Reg Strangeway started on the railway as a cleaner at Malton shed in February 1914 and retired from there in 1962, after 48 years. He worked on one of the steam coaches every other week for four years:

It had a boiler at one end and could be driven from either end. It worked like an ordinary steam engine but it was easier because you only had two levers. One was the reverser and the other was the throttle. In a neutral position you could take these levers out and take them to the other end. The fireman could sit down and would fire it with a small fireside shovel. The coal was at the side, and the seat next to it. The fireman put the coal down a tube, and he twisted his hand so as to distribute it evenly on the fire. He had to be careful not to get it stuck down the tube. If you had small enough coal it would go down. It was surprising how much coal they held - 8 or 10 hundredweight. The only thing you wanted was plenty of steam. *British Queen* was a good one, but the only trouble about it was that it didn't steam very well.

After the Malton/Gilling service ended in 1930 Sentinel steam railcars were used on the afternoon school trains from Pickering to Helmsley. Malton crews worked an afternoon train from Scarborough to Pickering via Seamer. Before returning to Scarborough they took the school train to Helmsley and back. Two-cylinder Sentinel 237 *Rodney* was used, but was later replaced by six-cylinder 2136 *Hope*. When the Pickering/Scarborough service ended in 1950 so too did the use of the Sentinels on the Ryedale lines, to be replaced by the push-and-pulls.

During the Second World War the D20s were moved to more important work, and LNER G5 0-4-4Ts were used on the truncated Pickering trains. In push-and-pull mode these engines also took over the Pickering to Helmsley school train after the withdrawal of the Sentinels. Two D17 4-4-0s were used immediately after the end of the War on the York/Pickering service. The final years of the service were entrusted mainly to D49 4-4-0 'Hunt' and 'Shire' Class locomotives, initially the former but from about 1951 the latter. The York/Pickering trains usually passed each other at Coxwold and their crews changed over there. On 31st January 1953, the last day of the passenger service, D49s 62730 *Westmorland* and 62735 *Berkshire* were in use.

The more powerful passenger locomotives were used on the Summer Saturday passenger trains to and from the east coast and on the Ampleforth College specials. Many V2 2-6-2 and B1 and B16 4-6-0 engines with long passenger trains found themselves trundling along the T&M at speeds of up to 30 m.p.h. Pacific classes A1, A2, A3 4-6-2 as well, but the most impressive sight of all was that of a streamlined A4. 60017 *Silver Fox* and 60026 *Sir Miles Beevor* were used on College specials in 1950, 1961 and 1963.

English Electric Type 4 (later Class 40) diesel locomotives were the only main line diesel to appear on the branches, on College specials, east coast trains and excursions. D258 was the first, working a special from Kirbymoorside to King's Cross in June 1962. Diesel multiple-units (DMUs) were increasingly used from 1959 for the College specials to and from Leeds, as well as on excursions. The last passenger trains to use any of the lines in July 1964 were DMUs.

On the goods trains, as the LNER took over the Class 398s were becoming obsolete and the larger Class J 0-6-0 tender locomotives took their place: J21, J24, J25 and J26. Former Hull and Barnsley J23s, based at Malton, also appeared. The first non-NER locomotives were the J39s, first recorded in 1943. In the final years the staple pickup locomotive was the J27 but ex-LMS locomotives and BR Standards were briefly used in the early 1960s.

Shunting at the stations often required

fly-shunting, a technique that was officially not allowed. The collected accounts of four train crew, Sandy Atkinson, Ron Benson, Reg Strangeway and George Arundale, explain:

A lot of stations had ropes and we should have roped them by, or shunted when we came the other way because we were really supposed to shunt in certain directions. But if someone was waiting for a wagon of coal, and it was going to be 7 or 8 hours before you came back, you either roped them by or fly shunted. At some stations there was a long siding running parallel to the main line. Wagons for each station were usually set at the right place in the train. We backed the whole train into this siding, then started forward again. The guard would be on the back of the engine, holding the grab rail with his left hand and the shunting pole in his right hand in between the coupling. He just nodded his head and the driver just shut the steam off and reversed the engine, so the wagons' buffers pressed up. The guard uncoupled the wagon and the driver went into forward gear again and was away. The fireman was on the ground and would change the points, and the porter would be ready with a brake stick to stop the wagon in the siding. Some of the guards were smart at that job but it was a co-operative effort.

Nunnington was tricky because it was on a hill. Shunting was carried out as we were travelling towards Helmsley. You had to have a lot of speed to knock a wagon off into the yard, but at one point in the yard there was a sudden fall. On one occasion we got going so fast to knock this wagon off that it came off the road. Later Nunnington's siding was in such bad repair that we couldn't fly shunt there.

The Wharram and Burdale stone trains – the 'chalkies' - demanded locomotives of additional power. In the 1920s LNER Class A7 4-6-2T Nos. 1175 and 1179 were used, based at Thirsk. In the 1940s the Q5 and Q6 0-8-0s were in common use on the chalkies as well as on wartime ammunition trains. Later O7 (later re-classified WD) 2-8-0s were allocated to the task but, as the stone traffic declined and the work was transferred to Malton shed, J27s and J39s were more usual.

Driving the chalkies presented a particular problem at Scarborough Road junction, where the T&M climbed at 1 in 55 from its junction with the M&D and passed over the York to Scarborough line. The trains had to slow down to exchange single line tablets and were therefore unable to take a run at the hill. The Scarborough Road occurrence book relates an occasional consequence as a train accelerated away from the junction and up the hill. This one happened in 1941:

Thirsk 'chalk' engine [Q6 0-8-0] 2273 with 12 wagons broke away from the rest of the train near the river bridge at 9.3 a.m. today. The rear portion was braked down to the junction and the front portion followed cautiously. In restarting, the hook broke off another wagon about 10th from the engine. The train was then set back and the defective wagons were 'knocked off' into the Bacon Factory siding. About 32 minutes' delay was incurred.

Reg Strangeway, long-time driver on the T&M, describes the problem and its solution:

When you were driving a train of 30 loose-coupled wagons of stone it needed a knack, which we at Malton had because we were used to driving these trains. Living near Scarborough Road, I could hear ever such a going on on that bank, especially when Thirsk-based men took the stone trains from Burdale. It was the noise of couplings tightening all down the train. They would get so far up but the wheels on the engine would start slipping, so they had to go back down onto the Driffield line and have another go. They used to break any number of couplings. The knack was this: as you came down the Driffield line and approached the junction, you braked so that all the buffers were together. You opened out just enough to make the couplings tight and then changed the tablet. Then you opened out properly to get up the hill.

On the closure of Malton shed in 1963 a Drewry Class 03 diesel shunting locomotive provided the pickup engine but for the last day of the Kirbymoorside pickup on 7 August 1964 J27 65894 was returned specially. Later this locomotive was preserved.

A4 Pacific Silver Fox *at Gilling on 10 April 1950, at the end of the Ampleforth College Easter term, forming the 8.23 a.m. to King's Cross via Sunbeck. The full panoply of Gilling's pre-1955 signals can be seen in the background. (Chris Wilson)*

19 - Events and Mishaps

The railways of Ryedale had their share of mishaps, some leading to fatalities. On 24 July 1911 the 8.35 a.m. pickup goods from Thirsk to Kirbymoorside was hauled by NER Class 398 0-6-0 374, Driver Renton and Guard Shepherd. The line from Sunbeck to Husthwaite Gate and Coxwold was on an almost continuous rising gradient. The Husthwaite Gate station master George Nathaniel Peacock described what happened next in the occurrence book:

At about 9.55 a.m. I heard the bell signal 'Vehicles Running Away'. On looking out I saw part of the train entering our station without an engine. I saw they were coming at a good speed but they were travelling faster than I could run. I managed to grasp the van however and succeeded in getting into the van (but in doing so the sudden jerk wrenched my arm and caused me to bruise my leg against the step, but I do not think I shall be much worse). I applied the brake of the van and got them stopped as soon as I could. The runaway portion consisted of 14 wagons and the guard's van.

Peacock received a monetary reward from the company and a letter of congratulation from his District Superintendent. A similar event happened on 18 April 1931. J.W. Marsh, the porter at Husthwaite Gate, made a vain attempt to board the train. Joyce Lawson, the daughter of Tommy Potter, the signalman at Sunbeck for more than 40 years, takes up the story: 'my father realised that he had to prevent the wagons from getting onto the main line. It was a Saturday and the main line was very busy. His first idea was to shovel some ballast onto the rails at Sunbeck and to pile it up in order to slow the wagons down. But he realised that they would be going at quite a speed and that it wouldn't be any use doing that. So he deliberately derailed the wagons'. Harold Burn, who lived nearby at Oak Farm, Pilmoor, saw it all: 'after the first four or five wagons had passed Sunbeck he threw the points and the rest of the train piled up. The first wagons did get away and finished up on the main line just south of Pilmoor station. The points were smashed up and there were quite big pieces of metal strewn around'.

On 9 August 1904 the 5.28 p.m. Pickering to York train was derailed when it split some points as it was leaving Gilling. A contemporary newspaper provides the detail:

All the occupants [of the second coach] mostly women and children, experienced a regular succession of violent 'bumps'. Some of them rushed to the windows to see what had happened, but before they had time to realise the situation the carriage turned over on its side, and the passengers in the different compartments fell 'all in heaps', as one of the unfortunate described it.

When the train was brought to a standstill… an extraordinary state of things was seen. On the main line stood the engine and the first carriage intact; lying across the two sets of rails on its side was the second coach; while the three remaining carriages were standing on the siding absolutely uninjured and not displaced. The occupants of the upstanding carriages at once dismounted. Not so the people in the overturned vehicle. There was just sufficient room for the passengers to crawl or be dragged out of the windows on the lower side. Great was the terror of the women and children in their perilous position. In the work of rescue their fellow passengers lent ready hands, and the liberated ones, more terror-stricken than hurt, were accompanied back to the station.

In November 1875 all nine vehicles – an empty horse box, a cattle wagon loaded with sheep, six coaches and a brake van - of the 9.15 p.m. Gilling to Pickering train were derailed rounding the bend at Cawton, where the G&P swung to the north away from the T&M. Three of the vehicles fell onto their sides but injuries to the 20 passengers were slight. The Board of Trade Inspector, Lieutenant-Colonel C.S Hutchinson, was unable to find a single cause and the track was in good condition.

There were many more derailments, most minor. At Slingsby on 24 January 1927 the 6.43 p.m. passenger train from Gilling to Malton detached a horse box into the dock. It was dark at the time. The signalman forgot to reverse the points for the main line but he gave the guard the signal to start. On seeing the guard's green hand signal the driver set off although the starting signal was at danger. The result was that the train ran along the up siding and became derailed at the wheel chock at the end. The reference in the occurrence book states that 'no-one seemed much the worse for the accident'. According to anecdote, there was only one passenger and he was drunk.

During the early 1950s the engine of a cattle train had become derailed at Kirbymoorside and a steam crane had rerailed it. After the work was done the crane was parked on the line up onto the coal depot. Keith Cass takes up the story:

Harry Young, the signalman, came hurtling up the platform. Normally he wasn't one for rushing about. I got him sat down in the chair by the fire. The crane had run away off the depot and was off down the line to Malton Road crossing. I got on the circuit phone to Mrs Magson there 'shut your gates and keep them shut'. 'Why?' 'There's a crane coming your way. Keep the gates shut, because it'll come back'. The thing went hurtling through, came to a rising gradient and then came back. I don't know how many times it did this, but it went through the gates more than once and stopped within sight of the depot. The loco that had become derailed was there for several days and when they came to take it away there wasn't a scrap of coal, or even dust, left in the tender, which is a sad reflection on Kirbymoorside and district.

Helmsley was the scene of a derailment on the wedding day of the Duke and Duchess of Kent on 8 June 1961. The wedding took place in York but the reception was at Hovingham, and three special trains conveyed the guests to Malton, all headed by A4 Pacifics. Two of the trains were parked on the M&D east of the level crossing at Malton East junction in Norton. Sandy Atkinson was the driver of the pickup that day, which set off from Malton an hour earlier than normal so as to get back to Malton before the line was closed for the wedding trains:

We were in Helmsley yard, which had a lot of hand points in the yard. As we were passing over one of these points we split them and went into the earth, all wheels. They couldn't use the Malton toolvans so they called out the Scarborough toolvans. They got us back on before the branch was closed that day because we went back light engine. But the Scarborough toolvans were stuck at Amotherby for several hours.

One of the fatal accidents to mar the T&M and G&P occurred at Ampleforth on 30 December 1865. A non-stop passenger train, known as the Scotch Express but, according to the Board of Trade report, 'frequently running without passengers', ran at speed into the station siding, burying itself in a mound of earth. The locomotive ran over and killed a bricklayer, John Bilton, who had gone to the station to collect some flooring tiles and was unloading them from a wagon in the siding.

On 20 June 1872 Thomas Thompson, the driver of the 7 a.m. passenger train from Malton to Thirsk, was killed at Slingsby. On the train stopping there he had taken an oil can and walked around the footplate, oiling several moving parts. On receiving the 'right away' the fireman set the train off but Thompson had either alighted or fallen off, and his head became jammed between a side rod and the engine.

A fatal accident at Scarborough Road junction (then known as Norton junction) occurred on Christmas Eve 1873, the first day of operation of the new signal cabin above the road bridge. Various railway officials were there to see that everything was working properly. The 11.10 a.m. Malton to Thirsk train, consisting of a horse-box, five carriages and a brake van, was setting off towards Thirsk. The facing points for the Thirsk line were out of sight under the bridge. Francis Boynton, a relief signalman who was under instruction, pulled the points back as the last two vehicles were passing over them. They were derailed and James Carr, a NER platelayer, was killed when, having jumped out as the carriage lurched to one side, it fell onto him.

The final fatal accident took place on 31 July 1961 at Fryton level crossing. Mrs Doris Gibbs had been the crossing keeper there since 1939. She was deaf and had been off duty sick for several days beforehand. There was some doubt as to whether a relief keeper had been called out that day. Be that as it may, the steam-hauled excursion train from Helmsley to Scarborough for the local Sunday Schools struck Mrs Gibbs as it passed. The crew of the train was unaware of the accident, which was only discovered by the driver of the pickup, Sandy Atkinson, as he came on the scene an hour or so later.

20 - People

Every railway had its quota of individuals who are remembered, mostly fondly, for many years afterwards. One of the best-remembered at Kirbymoorside was Jim Clark, the local carter, as was his white-bearded father Frank from 1906. The Clarks, father and son, had a contract with the NER and LNER to deliver and collect goods between the station and the town. Their horse-drawn rulley was a flat platform with a one-and-a-half-inch lip round it, with red wheels and spokes, a black band round the metal hub and a deep blue band with gold lettering: L.N.E.R. Jim was at the station first thing in the morning and for the last train at night for any perishables for the shops. Oswald Gillery, a clerk at the station, worked with Jim sheeting – listing – the parcels off the first train in the morning for delivery in the town: 'he would read the labels, getting his eyes quite close to them: "one 'cartoon' from Hemel Hempstead". Before you could get one finished he would start on the next one. You had the utmost difficulty in getting him to wait while you caught up'.

According to Mark Fairburn 'Jim himself was stone deaf but this didn't seem to matter: you just touched his cap or his shoulder to tell him you wanted him. Once you had got him you pointed to what you wanted shifted. He knew then what you meant'. In later years when Jim was, perhaps, not in the first flush of youthful vigour, the station master Herbert Dobson, told him of a parcel to be delivered. Jim said 'can I hug it?' 'Yes, that's all right', so Jim hugged it up the street, put it on his cart but then came back down to the station with the cart to collect something else. Vera Heath remembered Jim as 'a grand chap; he would do anything for me. He'd been there so long he knew what was expected, when it was expected and everything'.

Another occasion, remembered by Don Watson, was when a wagon of provisions for the Kirbymoorside shops was being unloaded: 'the warehouse had a platform which you could back a horse and rulley up to. There was a pile of big cartons of corn flakes. Jim was always in a rush and he got about four of these boxes of corn flakes piled right up in front of him. He couldn't see where he was going. However, the old horse had walked on about three yards, leaving a gap between the platform and the rulley. Jim Clark walked off the platform, carrying these boxes of corn flakes and of course he went head first down onto the ground. He didn't get hurt because he dropped on the boxes. It was very funny. Then he started thumping the horse when he got up!' Dick Potter, a signalman at Kirbymoorside, remembered that Jim's horse was named Charlie.

Roy Andrew knew him well too: 'there was an excursion to a football match at Middlesbrough so I thought I'd go. It left Kirbymoorside at about 11 o'clock. In an unwise moment I told Jim I was going on this excursion. And then Jim said he was going with his wife and I thought "I mustn't go in his carriage whatever I do". I dallied until the last moment and the guard was waving his flag when I ran round to the platform, only to find Jim with the carriage door wide open, waiting for me to get in. His wife was nearly as deaf as he was. It was a long time to Middlesbrough. I was hoarse! Coming back, I dodged him all right'.

Roy Andrew was a young man when he worked at Kirbymoorside towards the end of the First World War. One disturbing event happened which, by his own admission, taught him a valuable lesson:
I was collecting tickets from the dinnertime train and I noticed one man. The platform wasn't big enough for him. He was staggering about from one side to the other. He got in front of me, trying to find his ticket. He went through every pocket he had and at the finish I said 'get away. I haven't seen you'. I looked out of the office window. It was a bit of a breezy day and I saw him put his hand in his pocket and take a roll of pound notes out. Five or six of these blew out of his hand. So I dashed out and gathered up all the ones I could find and said to him 'put them in your pocket and just take one out now, while I'm watching'. Off he went but about an hour and a half later I looked out of the window again and I saw him coming down again, staggering about.

There wasn't a train until four o'clock, so he went and sat on a platform seat. About a quarter of an hour later a police sergeant came down. 'have you a strange character anywhere about here?' 'Yes, he's sat on the platform seat,' I said, 'he's as drunk as a lord'. He went up to him, and came back saying 'you must be very careful in your remarks about people, young man'. I said 'why?' 'That man isn't drunk. It's the worst case of shell shock I've seen. He has relatives in West End here, but he's not told them he's coming and they've gone off for the day. He's at a loose end now'. I had my sandwiches with me and the police sergeant brought him in and sat him down. I found that he talked quite naturally. I shared my sandwiches with him and made him a cup of tea, and then I left him. I gave him about 20 minutes on his own and then came back. 'Thank you very much,' he said, 'and thank you most of all for going out. If you'd stayed in I should have got hold of that cup of tea and it would have finished up on the ceiling. I've got no control at all, except when I'm on my own, when I don't think about it so much'. Six weeks after, exactly the same thing happened again. I said 'have you let them know you're coming?' 'No' he said, 'I can't write any more!' They weren't in, so back he came to me again and he had some of my lunch.

Tom Barlow was the station master at Gilling from 1916 until 1939. Dr J.P.T. Bury, whose father was the Rector of Gilling during almost the same period, recalled him as 'a short, portly, rather self-important man with ginger hair'. The memories of Wilfred Jackson of Cawton gatehouse were of Barlow travelling down the line on the goods pickup every week or two, to visit the other stations that came within his purview after 1926: 'he stood on the rear platform of the brake van, dressed like an admiral, with gold braid and finery, surveying his crew. We children used to salute him as he passed. You "paid a pound" to speak to Barlow, and waited until you were spoken to. You were conscious that he was in charge'. Arthur Cook, who was a clerk at Gilling in the 1920s, reckoned that Barlow 'had everybody scared stiff of him, especially the lad porters, but not me. He was a martinet and had a bad temper. When he got vexed the blood used to leave his lips and they went snow white. Joe Suggitt, the signalman, was also the Gilling village cobbler and he did all his cobbling work in the signal cabin. Barlow used to get mad at times but it made no difference and Joe kept on mending them there. I always said that, after you'd been at Gilling under Tommy Barlow, you could go anywhere.' Fred Pickering, whose father had been a track walker between Helmsley and Gilling, remembered Barlow the keen fisherman: 'the Holbeck runs through Gilling station. We would go and set night lines for the fish and we would be coming over the fields the next morning with a big

Bob Miller hands over the tablet to the fireman of a J39 0-6-0 after the completion of shunting operations at Husthwaite Gate, circa 1951/2. The short train then continued to Coxwold. (Author's Collection)

trout. Barlow used to go mad "I paid for a fishing licence to catch fish and you people go and get a fish like that!'" To the consternation of his successor, when he retired Barlow had a house built next to the level crossing at Gilling, in which he lived with his sister.

Mention of cobbling brings Bob Miller to mind: he was a platelayer and later a relief porter based at Gilling. During the Second World War 'the village cobblers from Gilling were both at the War and I was asked to do their work. They used to bring sacks full of these shoes from the College. I soled and heeled and charged 8/6d a pair. Years and years ago I used to watch a cobbler and that's how I picked a lot of it up. This all started when Mrs Barlow, the wife of the Coxwold crossing keeper Albert Barlow, saw some shoes that I'd cobbled for my wife and asked me to do hers. I was known all over'. Some thought little of the quality of Bob's work, however. Audrey Hugill was one: 'Mr Gillery, the station master, used to tip some of these shoes out to have a look at his work. I've never seen such terrible work!'

Geoff Fish was a clerk at Gilling during and after the Second World War. John Smithson, who started at the station in 1948, remembered that Geoff had difficulty in arriving at work on time: 'he came from Norton, where he lived, to Gilling. Sometimes he would catch a bus as far as Hovingham, because at that time the West Yorkshire bus terminated there. He kept an old bike in a shed in the Malt Shovel. It would often puncture or break down and so he'd either carry it or walk with it. Sometimes he would arrive on the back of a lorry. One time, a chauffeur-driven car arrived outside the office and out stepped Geoff; he'd hitched a lift. Another time you could see him walking across the fields - he'd got a lift as far as Stonegrave. At times latterly he would come unofficially with Walter Caygill, the motor driver from Malton'. Mrs Caygill confirmed this and added 'Geoff Fish was a big smoker and he put the window down when they were going along the road and the wind blew the sparks from the cigarette onto the wagon. Walter told me that Geoff kept looking out and back through the mirror, so he said "what's the matter, Geoff?" "I think we're on fire". He pulled up quickly as he had some cases of whisky on. Luckily there wasn't much damage done.'

There was a small orchestra at Gilling during the Second World War years, organised by Arthur Gillery, the son of the station master and then a schoolboy :

We gave concerts at Christmas, Easter and Whitsuntide. There were about six people in the orchestra. There were two first violins and two second violins, a cello and clarinet. Tom Inman, the relief signalman who lived in one of the railway cottages at Gilling, was one of the violins, as was a lad from Grimston. I played second violin. Jack Suggitt played the cello; Geoff Fish played the clarinet; Jack Smailes, who was the chief clerk,

Desmond Lee at the window of the Helmsley signal box, date unknown. The coal depot is on the left. (Author's Collection)

For the final years of the line the two men who ran Coxwold were the station master, Lewis Bradley, and the porter signalman, Cyril Sherwood. They are seen here on the platform of the station. (Geoff Dickson)

Above: Fred Wright was the porter signalman at Slingsby for 22 years from 1942. He is seen here amongst the paraphernalia of a country station office. The typical sloping railway office desk predominates. Top left is the lower edge of the office clock with the small hatch to the pendulum hanging down, as it so often did. Below it are pigeon holes for papers and circulars, with Fred's uniform cap hanging alongside. On the sloping desk lies the signal box train register, with the hand lamp behind. Hanging on the door right of centre is the parcels charging scale. On the right, top to bottom, are the framed plan of the Engineer's Rail Motors run-offs, various circulars in spring clips, a sweeping broom and the fireplace. (Author's Collection via Fred Wright)

Below: In 1916 several cannons were delivered to Kirbymoorside station. According to the NER Magazine of October 1916 they were German guns, formerly used against the natives of West Africa. They were presented to Captain Cyril Fuller R.N. (1874 - 1942), later Vice-Admiral Sir Cyril Fuller, who had taken a prominent part against the Germans in the Cameroons. The gun carriages are inscribed C.T.M.F. Kirbymoorside Yorkshire; they are on their way to Fuller's home at Douthwaite Hall. (Author's Collection)

played the piano. We practised in the school room but, if that was being used, my father used to let us use the station waiting room. Tom was a great friend of mine and we used to practise in the signal box, when he a had a minute between trains, and he would rattle away. He used to say, when I was off school or on a Saturday, 'bring the violin and we'll have a tune.' We got through lot of music.

Herbert Dobson was a clerk at Kirbymoorside from 1915 to 1932 and was its station master from 1942 until 1955, a total of 30 years, and he undoubtedly felt a strong affinity with the town. Amongst his many achievements he was the author of a series of humorous articles about a fictitious station master, John Goldbraid, in the North Eastern Railway Magazine and its successors. Vera Heath, who was a clerk there during the Second World War, concluded that 'he was a clever man, I think, worthy of better places than Kirbymoorside'. Like his counterparts elsewhere, as station master he had the coal sale. Keith Cass recalled him saying 'I've sold hundreds of tons of water in my time, Cass, hundreds of tons. I like it to rain'. (The rain increased the weight of the coal, so that less was needed to fulfil an order.)

Dobson was a crafty man. Keith Cass: 'District Office was always after you not to keep any spare wagons at the station, but everybody liked to keep a wagon or two up their sleeves. If you wanted a van in a hurry it took three days to get it, so we always had one or two in the yard. District Office used to send inspectors round. Mr Dobson would be sitting at his desk, and see the inspectors coming. As soon as they walked in through the doors he used to get his watch out and look at the clock, and he used to persuade them that, if they wanted to get back to York before the late evening, they should leave immediately. He would get his timetable out: 'I'll get my car out and if I run you to Sinnington, you'll be in time to catch the bus. You'll be back in York by two o'clock, otherwise it'll be eight tonight.' So they'd sign the stock book and then get into his car and he'd race them off in his car down to Sinnington. And they didn't notice the spare wagons that were in the yard and which they were supposed to check up on'.

For Betty Woodhouse, Dobson was quite a character:

If you gave him your best, he would tolerate a lot and be quite friendly. During the War we were very conscientious and I got on all right with him because I think I did an honest day's work. It wasn't often that Mr Dobson came out with remarks but I never forget that one day he came in and said 'Well, my wife's gone away for the day. So I can put my feet on the table and the frying pan on the mantle piece if I want to.' You couldn't imagine the man considering doing anything like that even if he had free licence to do it. Normally he was without his teeth and his gums were so hard that they could grip his pipe. Talking now I can virtually hear him drawing on his pipe.

You could chronicle Herbert Dobson's movements: from his house and into the office he would come and you could hear his footsteps. If we

The final passenger-carrying train to run to Kirbymoorside was the Ramblers' Excursion on 3 May 1964, seen here crossing Kirkdale viaduct. (John Spencer Gilks)

were having a five minute breather we had to start work again. He used to put on his 'silent boots' sometimes, and go out into the yard and find the porters skiving, lying down in the warehouse and having a chat.

Dobson was also associated with the occasion on 27 November 1950 when his dignity was somewhat affronted. Keith Cass:

Malton Road crossing was a mile from the station. On one occasion the morning train to Pickering had a driver that didn't know the road terribly well. There was thick fog and Dobson decided that he would ride with the driver as a pilotman, and would come back on the bus from Pickering. He told me to phone Mrs Magson, the crossing keeper, and tell her that the train was leaving and that she must open the gates now. I got an earful from Mrs Magson but I'd done as I was told. He'd said to the driver 'exactly one mile ahead - not an inch more nor less - is a set of gates'. 'I know the gates'. Off they set and about a quarter of an hour after the train had left Dobson returned, half running along the platform, and came racing into the office, to ring Control. They had run through the gates at Malton Road crossing; it was quite a kerfuffle and embarrassing to him. He was absolutely livid!

The auditors were the bane of station clerks' lives and their visits were dreaded. Some auditors were more fearsome than others. Leslie Oldfield, a clerk at Kirbymoorside in the late 1930s, remembered them as being very strict: 'before the War it was George Hall. It used to be on the bush telegraph that he was coming. If you saw him coming off the train you did a quick shuffle round and made sure everything was tidy. In those days the station master also ran the coal business and we often had his money in tins with the station money. As soon as we heard he was coming we took all the coal and other money out of the cash drawer. He used to sit on a high stool: 'get me the cash book. Get me this; get me that', and we would do it. He would weigh and charge every parcel that came in, and work out the overcharges and undercharges. Even if there was a parcel from, say, Birmingham which had been undercharged by

The last passenger trains of all on the Ryedale lines were the Sunday School excursions to Scarborough on 27 July 1964. The second, from Gilling, is seen here approaching Scarborough Road junction. (Author)

The last train was hauled by former NER J27 0-6-0 No. 65894. An addiitonal brake van was added to accommodate a party of enthusiasts. The train is seen at Kirbymoorside. (Ken Hoole)

sixpence we had to clear it and apply to the sender for the extra amount'. When the passenger service had finished in 1953, the auditor came by the Reliance bus. The porter signalman at Gilling, Gilbert Hugill over whose level crossing the bus ran, would sometimes spot the familiar face and telephone through to Helmsley. Very useful!

21 The End

After the regular passenger services were withdrawn in January 1953 the only passenger trains that served the remaining stations on the T&M and G&P were those described earlier: to and from the coast, for Ampleforth College, and excursions. The G&P level crossings at Harome Siding, Pockley Gates and Starfitt Lane were unmanned, but when special passenger trains were run a locally-resident platelayer attended to the gates. As far as goods traffic was concerned, there was the daily pickup and regular trains of limestone from Burdale, Thornton Dale and Hovingham.

In the late 1950s the management of British Railways' North Eastern Region was agonising about the future of the lines. A plan in 1960 to convert the Pilmoor to Gilling section into a light railway was abandoned when it was pointed out that the summer Saturday passenger trains to and from the coast would have to travel via York. In 1961 discussions took place with the West Yorkshire Road Car Co. regarding conveying Ampleforth College students by bus to and from York.

The run-down of traffic on the T&M was inexorable. The last train of stone to Thirsk ran on 3 February 1962. Between Husthwaite Gate and Pilmoor there were no more goods trains; the only passenger trains to traverse the whole T&M that year were three excursions, 18 drivers' route-learning specials and 59 summer Saturday trains to and from the coast. That year the North Eastern Region's Chief Signal and Telegraph engineer warned that the Ryedale lines' telegraph system was at risk of breaking down. The management decided that summer 1962 would *probably* be the last when the summer Saturday trains travelled via the T&M. Sunbeck was closed for the winter and, as it turned out, for ever on October 5 1962. The last movement to pass the signal box had been an Engineer's Rail Motor on 19 September 1962 but it did not pass onto the main line. Attendance was withdrawn from Ampleforth level crossing on 17 December 1962. During the night of 19 March 1963 a parcels train was derailed at Pilmoor and destroyed the T&M junction. It was quickly decided not to replace it and the line between Pilmoor and Husthwaite Gate was closed; a wheel-chock was placed across the line a few yards west of the latter station. In order to enable the goods pickup to travel from Coxwold to Husthwaite Gate without opening Sunbeck signal box, a tablet was kept out of the machine at Coxwold for the remaining 17 months' life of the railways.

On 29 April 1964 the rail staff negotiating body,

Finally, reference has been made many times in this narrative to five young women who worked at Helmsley, Nawton and Kirbymoorside during the 1940s and who, confusingly, possessed overlapping maiden and married names. They are: Betty Armstrong/Woodhouse, Rene Armstrong/Armstrong, Olive Burn/Wrightson, Betty Otterburn/Watson, Vera Watson/Heath.

the Sectional Council, was informed that the Ryedale lines would be closed that summer. The annual revenue was given as £25,269, of which £22,262 would be lost on closure. However, the savings of £37,353 on movements, £14,269 on engineering and £53,582 on staff greatly outweighed that. Coal customers asked that they be given a chance to stock up for the winter.

The date of 10 August was agreed for closure, except between Amotherby and Malton because of a long-term contract with the Brandsby Agricultural and Trading Association. The last College special ran via Malton on Tuesday 28 April, the last Ramblers' Excursion on Sunday 3 May. Appropriately, the last passenger trains to use the T&M and G&P were for the local communities: Sunday School excursions on Monday 27 July 1964. A diesel multiple-unit train was organised by the Helmsley Sunday Schools, but demand for seats was so great that a second train had to be laid on, organised by the Slingsby Sunday Schools. The six-car Helmsley train left at 8 a.m. and ran non-stop from Gilling, apart from the necessary reversals at Scarborough Road and Malton. The seven-car Gilling train departed at 8.39 and called at Hovingham, Slingsby, Barton-le-Street and Amotherby. The two trains arrived at Scarborough at 9.25 and 9.52 respectively. The return trains set off from Scarborough at 5.45 p.m. and 6.50 p.m., arriving at Helmsley and Gilling at 7.12 and 8.01 respectively. The last pickup ran to Kirbymoorside and Husthwaite Gate on Friday 7 August 1964. The Amotherby to Scarborough Road portion of the T&M was closed ten weeks later on 16 October, with the last ever revenue movement over the line arriving back at Scarborough Road at 2.14 p.m. that day.

Track removal started on 29 March 1965 at Kirbymoorside and on 20 April at Sunbeck. A diesel shunting engine was used, with a driver, second man, guard and engineer. Most of the signals had been removed by then and the crew worked the level crossing gates, and the points at Scarborough Road and the stations. A stretch of fairly new track was left in situ near the A19 Thormanby Bridge and was removed later. Gilling was reached in mid-June. Most of the iron underbridges were cut up by gangs working behind the demolition train.

The last piece of track was removed on 9 August 1965. Demolition of the Derwent viaduct was started on 22 August. The bridge over the York to Scarborough railway was removed on Sunday 19 September 1965. Thus ended the life of the Railways of Ryedale.

A worker surveys the desolate scene at Kirbymoorside station in early April 1965 as the track is removed. (Author's Collection)

Not good for running on - track about to be removed near Helmsley. (Author)

Sleepers being loaded at Nunnington on 29 May 1965, the station in the background. (Author)

Left: Track removal at Hovingham on 10 July 1965. The tank wagon carries fuel for the machinery. (Author)

Below: The bridge over the River Derwent was removed in August 1965. (Author)

Key Facts

Formal openings:
Sessay Wood junction - Malton Scarborough Road junction 19 May 1853. Bishophouse junction - Sunbeck junction 9 October 1871. Gilling - Helmsley 9 October 1871. Helmsley – Kirbymoorside 1 January 1874. Kirbymoorside - Pickering Mill Lane junction 1 April 1875.

Line closings: (note 1)
Pilmoor (Sessay Wood) junction - Husthwaite Gate 19 March 1963 (2). Bishophouse junction - Sunbeck junction 15 February 1959 (3). Husthwaite Gate – Amotherby Monday 10 August 1964. Amotherby - Malton Scarborough Road junction Monday 19 October 1964. Gilling – Kirbymoorside Monday 10 August 1964. Kirbymoorside - Pickering Mill Lane junction Monday 2 February 1953.

Stations:	Opened	Last day of service Passenger	Goods	Last passenger train to call
Husthwaite Gate	28 May 1854 (4)	31 Jan 1953	7 Aug 1964	28 Jun 1962
Coxwold	19 May 1853	31 Jan 1953	7 Aug 1964	1 Oct 1963
Ampleforth	19 May 1853	3 Jun 1950	3 Jun 1950	5 Jun 1950
Gilling	19 May 1853	31 Jan 1953	7 Aug 1964	27 Jul 1964
Hovingham Spa	19 May 1853	31 Dec 1930	7 Aug 1964	27 Jul 1964
Slingsby	19 May 1853	31 Dec 1930	7 Aug 1964	27 Jul 1964
Barton-le-Street	19 May 1853	31 Dec 1930	7 Aug 1964	27 Jul 1964
Amotherby	19 May 1853	31 Dec 1930	16 Oct 1964	27 Jul 1964
Nunnington	9 Oct 1871	31 Jan 1953	7 Aug 1964	25 May 1963
Helmsley	9 Oct 1871	31 Jan 1953	7 Aug 1964	27 Jul 1964
Nawton	1 Jan 1874	31 Jan 1953	7 Aug 1964	3 May 1964
Kirbymoorside	1 Jan 1874	31 Jan 1953	7 Aug 1964	3 May 1964
Sinnington	1 Apr 1875	31 Jan 1953	31 Jan 1953	31 Jan 1953